What a Jew does with Jesus

by
Art Katz

BURNING BUSH PRESS
BEMIDJI, MINNESOTA, USA

WHAT A JEW DOES WITH JESUS

by Art Katz

These and other materials of a comparable kind can be found at:

www.artkatzministries.org

ISBN 10 digit: 0-9749631-3-5
ISBN 13 digit: 978-0-9749631-3-6

Published by Burning Bush Press

First American Edition, 2008

About The Author

Art Katz was born in Brooklyn, New York, of Jewish parents, and grew up through the depression years and turbulence of World War II. Through his merchant marine and military experiences, and having embraced Marxist and existentialist ideologies, Art, now a teacher, was brought to a final moral crisis—able to raise the questions, but not able to answer the groaning perplexities of this modern age.

During a leave of absence and on a hitchhiking odyssey through Europe and the Middle East, the cynical and unbelieving atheist, vehement anti-religionist and anti-Christian, was radically apprehended by a God who was actively seeking him. The actual journal of that experience, *Ben Israel – Odyssey of a Modern Jew*, recounts Art's quest for the true meaning to life, which climaxed significantly and symbolically in Jerusalem.

Art attended Santa Monica City College, UCLA, and the University of California at Berkeley, earning Bachelor's and Master's degrees in history, as well as a Master's degree in theology at Luther Seminary, St. Paul, MN. With his speaking ministry spanning nearly forty years, Art sought to bring the radical relevance of the Bible's message to contemporary societies, both secular and religious. With several of his books translated into major foreign languages, Art traveled frequently and widely as a conference speaker and prophetic voice for the church until his death in 2007.

Acknowledgments

While delving through an old cardboard box in Art Katz's office, we discovered the faded, type-written pages of a manuscript on the theme of salvation, written by Art in about 1973. Recognizing the value of its contents, we initiated the effort to prepare the manuscript for publishing. As an addendum, we added Art's more recent article written in 2003, entitled: *The Chosen People – Chosen for What?*

Our appreciation goes out to those who helped with this task, with special thanks to Edith Crim for her integrity in carefully re-typing the whole document into a usable digital format, and for her keen editorial input. To Jeannie Clink we owe the bulk of the editing detail, undertaken with her usual buoyant willingness to volunteer her skills, coupled with her watchful eye for correct grammatical detail. We were able to draw on Chuck Schmitt for his symbolic artwork, and who himself had the highest regard for Art's evangelistic and prophetic burden. Not least, we want to thank those faithful friends, both Jewish and Gentile, who contributed financially to the publication costs.

Our prayer is that a fruit for the Kingdom would be reaped, one far greater than Art could ever have imagined when he first scribbled down his thoughts all those years ago, not knowing that they would one day be published posthumously. We dedicate this book to those dear Jewish souls brave enough to face the enigma and the seeming contradiction with which Jesus of Nazareth confronts them.

Simon Hensman
Laporte, MN
June 2008

WHAT A JEW DOES WITH JESUS

TABLE OF CONTENTS

ADDENDUM

• If There is a God, Where is He Now?
• The Jewish Predicament
• The Undoing of Pride
• The Rejection of God
• God's Answer to the Jewish Predicament
• Grace and Law
• The Consequences of Rejecting God
• The Consequences of Believing God
• A Final Prophetic Consideration
• A Prayer

INTRODUCTION

"Jews for Jesus"? Can anything sound more ridiculous? At the first hearing, one wonders if this is not some kind of joke, a dull-witted attempt to find humor in the apparently irreconcilable. Anyone with even the most rudimentary knowledge of Jewish history knows that from the Middle Ages to modern times, from the Crusades through the Inquisition till the Holocaust, that the name Jesus Christ, or the word *Christianity*, has been a source of sorrow and pain for Jewish life. How then can such a phenomenon as "Jews for Jesus" have come about? How can a Jew express any kind of affinity for this Jesus from Galilee, in whose name we have suffered so much?

Even the media attests to such an affinity being increasingly the case! What began first as a trickle of comment about Jews being part of the larger *Jesus Movement* became, in time, major national articles about the "Jews for Jesus" groups in themselves. Time Magazine[1] described them as "part of the growing, nationwide Jewish wing of the Jesus Movement." However difficult it is to categorize them, the article went on to attempt to assess the group's size and significance: "The young Jewish Christians are increasingly conspicuous. Their number, while modest compared with

---

[1] June 12, 1972 issue

the Jesus Movement as a whole, is unprecedented among U.S. Jews." Since then, reports indicate that what was once considered a trickle is in the process of becoming an ever-widening stream in the nations where Jews of every age and background are found.

Something is happening which is indeed unprecedented, and which cannot be shrugged off and dismissed from Jewish consciousness and consideration. The American Jewish Committee has had to acknowledge the phenomenon with a memo to its national branches. The entire issue of *Davka*,[2] a California Hillel publication, was given over to an examination of Jesus and the theological questions He provokes in Jews. Increasingly, volumes of articles are being written by rabbis, Jewish professors of religion, and other community leaders in response to this apparent *problem*. More disconcertingly, these Jews who say they 'believe in Jesus' assert that they have not for-saken being Jews, but on the contrary, they claim that their faith in Jesus has actually enhanced and deepened their Jewishness!

To the Jewish mind, the phenomenon of *conversion* has historically been understood as that cynical process of accommodation by which one changed one's religion to 'Christian' in order to escape the discrimination and trials that attended being Jewish. More often, as was the case with Karl Marx's family, it was considered a doorway to emancipation and increased opportunity among the Gentiles to whom they were already largely assimilated. This practice, rightfully odious to Jews, had nothing to do with belief, faith or convictions, such matters being as absent after the conversion as they were before. Not so, however, with today's Jews for Jesus; for as the Time Magazine article went on to explain, "Their most controversial claim is that they are still Jews, even though

---

[2] March-April issue, 1972

they now accept Jesus as the Messiah, promised by the biblical prophets. Many reject the label *convert*, and even Christian, preferring to call themselves *messianic* or *completed* Jews."

Can one be a Jew and still believe in Jesus? Does Jesus fulfill biblical prophecy of the promised Messiah? Martin (Moishe) Rosen, former leader of the San Francisco centered *Jews for Jesus* group says, "The traditional, rabbinical Judaism we know is not the religion delivered by God to the prophets. The Judaism of the prophets was founded on the basis of supernatural revelation...What kind of personal experience with God can the establishment-type Judaism offer to take the place of what we know has happened to us?" What confirming experiences with God do these Jewish believers profess to have? What evidence is there in changed lives and character that bespeaks an encounter with a living God?

However accomplished Jews may be in every field of intellectual and cultural endeavor, our biblical illiteracy is readily acknowledged. Marc Tannenbaum, rabbi in charge of inter-religious affairs for a rabbinical council, described the encounter between believing and unbelieving young Jews as "Christian biblical literalism confronting Jewish biblical illiteracy."[3] How many of us, who call ourselves intellectual, have satisfied ourselves with mere hearsay concerning God, the Bible and other matters of eternal consequence. We don't seem to be willing to undertake even a minimal investigation. Real seekers after truth will spare nothing in their painstaking search. How many of us who profess to be such seekers have blithely dismissed the person of Jesus without so much as a cursory examination, content instead to rest upon cheap platitudes and ignorant disdain?

This book is an attempt to set forth answers to these

---

[3] Time Magazine, June 12th 1972, p. 67

questions by a systematic review of the scriptures. We will be drawing upon our own experiences as believers, and the testimonies of other Jews known to us who, like us, "have found Him of whom Moses in the Law and the prophets did write."

CHAPTER 1

THE TWO JUDAISMS

Do not cast me away from Your presence and do not take your Holy Spirit from me.[1]

By whatever name, religion for most men in the world today seems to be overwhelmingly devoid of the Holy Spirit of God—be it howsoever sincere and well-meaning, be it Jewish or Gentile. From the above Scripture, does not the psalmist suggest that the life of God by His Spirit can actually be experienced, and that God's Presence can actually be known? But instead, is not the absence of this life-giving Spirit more the norm in our conventional lives? Can our religious ceremonies, our hallowed traditions, and our eloquent culture substitute for this life-giving provision of God?

We are saying that the Judaism that really is of God must necessarily be a Judaism of life. And that this life has its inception when an individual is brought into an actual life-union with God. The presence to which the psalmist

---

[1] Psalms 51:11

alluded must have been a real presence. The same Spirit who was "moving over the surface of the waters"[2] is referred to throughout all the scriptures as that life-giving aspect of God who "strives with men,"[3] is imparted to men,[4] and dwells in men.[5] "God is a Spirit," Jesus said, "and they that worship Him must worship Him in spirit and in truth."[6]   Anything less than this must surely be the Judaism of men—however frequent their mention of God, however time-honored their practices, and however correct their doctrines.   We are not here disputing the beauty of liturgy, nor the 'good-feelings' participants derive from synagogue or church services, nor the value such things have in reinforcing certain ethical values and preserving desirable cultures; let all these things be so and the Living God be absent, and tragically, we will have missed the true reality that is summed up in the word *Life*.

We appeal to the reader to picture a world in which mankind's first priority is living their lives unto themselves. In such a society, 'religion' must necessarily become a cultural-social appendage to which men give only nominal assent, and which they undertake in direct proportion to the requirement of social pressures and the availability of leisure time left to one *after* life's more 'earnest' pursuits are taken care of. For most of us Jews, religion is a means whereby we can affirm our Jewish identity and enjoy the pleasure of things familiar and often unique to ourselves. For many, if not most of our rabbis, is not God no more than a *concept*, an amorphous *higher power*, an embellishment for our Jewish lives to which we decorously refer on occasion, but who has the good sense not to impose Himself upon us any further? To profess to

---

[2]   Genesis 1:2b
[3]   Genesis 6:3
[4]   Numbers 11:17
[5]   Numbers 27:18
[6]   John 4:24

know Him would be considered extreme spiritual *chutzpah*; and to lay to heart the divine admonition, "you will seek Me and find Me when you search for Me with all your heart"[7] would be considered an embarrassment in the least, and fanaticism on the part of anyone who actually persisted in it.

How much then of what we see practiced in religious institutions is no more than a kind of ethical humanism—actually devoid of the presence, power and will of God, but larded over with impressive intonations and a suitable religious vocabulary? There seems to be very few examples of those who can say with the converted Jew, the apostle Paul, "in Him we live and move and exist."[8] Fewer yet can understand the Lord's invitation to abide in Him, and He in us: "As the branch cannot bear fruit of itself unless it abides in the vine, so neither can you unless you abide in Me."[9] This is no New Testament deviation from Old Testament practice, but the same God affirming the one way—the centrality of God in the life of the believer, which is at the heart of the very Judaism of God. Consider the God who speaks to us through the prophet Jeremiah:

> Thus says the Lord, "Cursed is the man who trusts in mankind and makes flesh his strength, and whose heart turns away from the LORD. For he will be like a bush in the desert and will not see when prosperity comes, but will live in stony wastes in the wilderness, a land of salt without inhabitant.
>
> Blessed is the man who trusts in the LORD and whose trust is the LORD. For he will be like a tree planted by the water, that extends its roots by a stream and will not fear when the heat comes; but its leaves will be green, and it will

---

[7] Jeremiah 29:13
[8] Acts 17:28
[9] John 15:4

not be anxious in a year of drought nor cease to
yield fruit."[10]

But what is the actual faith, trust and commitment that
we are to have in God for the whole substance of our lives
that is intimated in these scriptures? Do we know the life
of the Spirit, who effectually causes our anxious and
deepest fears to subside, as is evident in those who trust the
Lord? Would our cry, like the psalmist's, be an anguished
cry if that Spirit and Presence were taken from us?
Anything else by whatever name can justifiably be called
mere religion, and more than we know, an assertion of the
actual supremacy of man, no matter what position we give
God verbally. It is not much more than what William Law
describes as "a proud atheism of self, which has rejected
God as its only life and power."[11]

In the purposes of God, such a vital life-union with
Him is apparently wholly dependent on the voluntary free-
will of the individual to enter into it. While most men will
tolerate a measure of religion in their lives, fewer would be
willing to entertain an ongoing relationship with a holy
God who calls Himself a "consuming fire." This may well
be why the religions of convenience, or if you will, the
Judaisms of men, Jewish or Gentile, are preferred to the
biblical Judaism. It is our purpose to set forth the
principles of the latter in order to help the reader who
quests for reality and life to find its source—despite the
maze of conflicting claims and appeals to ones loyalties
and allegiances. It requires a heart that has set itself to
diligently seek Him: to "...love the Lord your God with all
your heart and with all your soul and with all your
might,"[12] and to "...have no other gods before Me."[13]

---

[10] Jeremiah 17:5-8
[11] Wm. Law, *The Power of the Spirit*. Page 141.
[12] Deuteronomy 6:5
[13] Deuteronomy 5:7

What is biblical Judaism?

There is perhaps no word more distorted in modern usage, than the word *faith*. Sadly, it has come to mean anything to which mankind gives nominal or mental assent. Any body of conviction or doctrine of which they approve now falls under this generic label. Others would speak of 'believing in God' as the acknowledgment that somehow and somewhere He exists! However, we feel that this is not doing justice to the faith spoken of in the scriptures. Indeed, if the scriptures assert that "without faith it is impossible to please Him,"[14] then it behooves us to leave no stone unturned in seeking out the true, God-intentioned meaning of this word and the reality that it implies.

One classic illustration of biblical faith is afforded us in the example of the father of faith, the patriarch Abraham, whose faith is set forth in the New Testament scriptures as the quintessential faith for all who will believe: "the faith of Abraham, who is the father of us all."[15]

> As it is written, "A father of many nations have I made you" in the presence of Him whom he believed, even God, who gives life to the dead and calls into being that which does not exist. In hope against hope he believed, so that he might become a father of many nations according to that which had been spoken...[16]

What essential principles of biblical Judaism do these scriptures express here? First, to believe God is to believe, "as it is written." This was the phrase with which Jesus prefaced many of His statements to His contemporaries, and, as we will soon show, He everywhere evidenced His

---

[14] Hebrews 11:6
[15] Romans 4:16f
[16] Romans 4:17-18

complete conviction that the scriptures were the inspired word of God and the revelation of God's will upon which men should stake their lives, and by which they should live. Often, however, this word is at variance with appearances and even opposed to our human reason. Thus, God requires that we *believe*, that is, that we act upon it with a trust and confidence in the character and integrity of Him who speaks it.

In the text quoted, this is exactly the case. God's word came to Abraham in his ninety-ninth year, at a time past any natural hope of its fulfillment, "I have made you the father of a multitude of nations."[17] Notice that He spoke in the past tense, though in advance of its realization.[18] Abraham's response was to believe God, a God "who gives life to the dead." This is no mere God of abstraction or concept, but a God who speaks, a God who promises, a God who has power to perform His word, and the God of resurrection! Abraham was "fully assured that what God had promised, He was able to perform,"[19] and we read, "Therefore it was also credited to him as righteousness."[20]

This supreme act of faith in the word of God, which is trust in the character of Him who spoke, opened a channel by which Abraham could receive the righteousness of God. Here we have another essential principle of biblical Judaism with which the Judaisms of the world are at variance, namely, that the righteousness of God can never be the result of man's own endeavor, but only through faith can we be made partakers of the Divine nature, which alone is righteous. Further, every man operating from the root of self inescapably corrupts even the most benevolent acts, because in every aspect of our life and being, God must be the source of our life and all that we do. Do we agree with

---

[17]   Genesis 17:5b
[18]   See Genesis 17:1-8
[19]   Romans 4:21
[20]   Romans 4:22

God's testimony of man, even man at his best, that there is "no one who does good, not even one"[21] and that "all have sinned and fall short of the glory of God"[22]?

Wherever man exalts himself, or points outside of himself to explain his character defects, or looks to himself for the ultimate solution of his troubles, we have the wisdom of man being expressed—even though it might be laced with the ceremonial sounds of seeming humility and contrition. Here is perhaps the immediate test for modern mankind in quest of the biblical God—when our subjective impression assures us that we are not so bad, at least better than most. But the word of God again and again instructs us that "all our righteous deeds are like a filthy garment"[23] and that "there is not a righteous man on earth who continually does good and who never sins."[24]

Which will we choose to believe—the notion of our own virtue, or the clear and repeated assertions of God about our fallen condition? The first states that we have no need of Him, the latter requires an entire dependence *upon* Him; the first keeps us on the treadmill of establishing our own petty kingdoms, the latter requires a repentant casting one's self upon God alone. In summarizing the life of Abraham, some of the key distinctions between the Judaism of God and that of men are:

1. Biblical Judaism portrays a God who is a person, who speaks and who makes a promise that He has the power to fulfill and the integrity to honor.

2. Biblical Judaism repeatedly describes a mankind that is fallen, selfish, sinful, at variance with God, and in need of redemption.

3. God, alone, who is the source of all righteousness,

---

[21] Psalms 53:3b
[22] Romans 3:23
[23] Isaiah 64:6b
[24] Ecclesiastes 7:20

is alone able to alter our condition. He alone calls into being that which does not exist.

4. Only a faith that is active and real, which, in believing the words of God, believes God Himself, can receive this, and indeed every gift of God.

> Now not for his sake only was it written that it was credited to him, but for our sake also, to whom it will be credited, as those who believe in Him who raised Jesus our Lord from the dead, He who was delivered over because of our transgressions, and was raised because of our justification.[25]

---

[25] Romans 4:23-25

CHAPTER 2

THE CLASH OF TWO JUDAISMS

Nowhere is the innate antipathy and inevitable clash of the two Judaisms better described than in the New Testament accounts themselves. Contrary to the popular impressions and oft-repeated banalities of many of my Jewish kinsmen, we maintain that Jesus was not a *reformer* whose opposition to the *status quo* resulted in His unfortunate death. Nor did He observe the prevailing Judaistic practices. On the contrary, He almost seemed to violate these practices. Nearly every word He spoke and every deed He performed brought Him the censure of His religious contemporaries. It seems that He was then, as He is now, a nuisance, an irritant, and a provocative revealer of men's thoughts and the intent of their hearts. Some loved Him, others hated Him; some worshipped Him, others cursed Him; some called Him deceiver, drunkard and demon-possessed while others called Him "Lord"; some taunted Him, others followed Him. Nothing has changed; it is the same now as it was then.

Any attempt by us to pass Him off as a *Jewish teacher*, a *good man*, or a *reformer* may well be the result of a willful ignorance that chooses to escape the profound challenge of His life and utterances. His every word and deed was in perfect compliance with a *biblical* Judaism, which brought Him invariably into conflict and reproach with the rabbinical, Talmudic Judaism of His time—and even this present time.

Indeed, He Himself said, "Do not think that I came to bring peace on the earth; I did not come to bring peace, but a sword."[1]   Because of what He represented, a man would be set "against his father, and a daughter against her mother...and a man's enemies will be the members of his household."[2]   In contrast, how much of our acknowledgment and seeming tribute to Jesus as *master*, or *rabbi*, indeed even *prophet*, are not much more than a patronizing pat that effectively dismisses Him as an issue for our lives?   Don't these dismissals contribute to, and even allow, the uninterrupted continuance of the *Judaism of men* rather than open the way for the true Judaism of God?

The Rich Young Ruler

A wonderful illustration of the clash of Judaisms is given in this encounter between Jesus and a certain young ruler who addresses Jesus as "Good Teacher."

> As He was setting out on a journey, a man ran up to Him and knelt before Him, and asked Him, "Good Teacher, what shall I do to inherit eternal life?"
>
> And Jesus said to him, "Why do you call Me good? No one is good except God alone. You know the commandments, 'DO NOT MURDER, DO NOT COMMIT ADULTERY, DO NOT STEAL, DO NOT BEAR FALSE

---

[1] Matthew 10:34
[2] Ibid., vv. 35-36

WITNESS, Do not defraud, HONOR YOUR FATHER AND MOTHER.' "

And he said to Him, "Teacher, I have kept all these things from my youth up." Looking at him, Jesus felt a love for him and said to him, "One thing you lack: go and sell all you possess and give to the poor, and you will have treasure in heaven; and come, follow Me."

But at these words he was saddened, and he went away grieving, for he was one who owned much property.[3]

Note that Jesus said to him, "Why do you call Me good? No one is good except God alone." Setting aside, for the moment, the important question of whether Jesus saw Himself as being equal to God, focus your attention on the fact that He perfectly subscribed to the biblical principle that "There is no one who does good, not even one."[4]

The young man had indeed asked the ultimate question: "What shall I do to inherit eternal life?" For those readers who are not occupied with such considerations, or who cannot believe that there is an eternity, note also that Jesus does not demean or ignore the matter, but gives full acknowledgment of its validity and importance by encouraging him to have "treasure in heaven."

Contrary to popular misconceptions, Jesus does not set aside the commandments of God; rather, unlike most men who are satisfied with only *trying*, in addressing the young ruler, He *expects* the commandments to be fulfilled. We can see here a vital difference between the Judaisms of men and the Judaism of God, namely, the standard by which we live our lives. As can be expected, the standards of men are

---

[3] Mark 10:17- 22
[4] Psalms 53:3

far less demanding and at enormous variance with the repeated biblical injunctions to "Walk before Me, and be blameless,"[5] or "You shall be blameless before the Lord your God."[6]

Perhaps man's most frequent sin is that of attempting to conform God to his own image. Irrespective of what Scripture repeatedly affirms, we imagine that He *must* be a reasonable God who surely gives an 'A' for effort! One of the greatest evidences of the cancer of sin in our lives is the deterioration of conscience, which enables us to be perfectly assured that God is satisfied with us, even though we have been indifferent to Him all our lives; neither have we really troubled ourselves to inquire what He expects of us.

In nothing are we so much self-confident as in our own self-righteousness. How many of us are even prepared to establish, in our sick and distraught generation, the building of brave new worlds, while daily we fail at civility, courtesy and self-control? Be assured that "The way of a fool is right in his own eyes"[7] and "There is a way *which seems* right to a man, but its end is the way of death."[8] And the Lord declares, "For My thoughts are not your thoughts, nor are your ways My ways."[9]

Should we not all the more look to the reply of Jesus, who is evidently less of an offense to God than we are?

After He had spoken to the young ruler, we read, "But at these words he was saddened, and he went away grieving, for he was one who owned much property."[10]

He could not part with the things he coveted in order to gain the Kingdom of God, but like the multitudes, he

---

[5] Genesis 17:1f
[6] Deuteronomy 18:13
[7] Proverbs 12:15a
[8] Proverbs 14:12 – emphasis mine
[9] Isaiah 55:8
[10] Mark 10:22

preferred a Judaism in which he could retain the right to all he had.   In contrast, the Judaism of God is radically different—demanding total commitment.   It is a Judaism of the *whole heart*; it asks of us "*all* our heart, *all* our soul, and *all* our might."[11]   This *all* is for *our* sake, to save *us* from the idolatries that would degrade and destroy us.   No wonder the Creator demands that He come first—enthroned as the God of our lives!   Ironically, our unwillingness to make Him Lord of our lives, keeps us from the one thing that can save us—the Judaism that is of God and life!

The Call of Abraham

In God's dealings with Abraham, we see the unchangeableness of God and the requirement of His way. In the Book of Beginnings we read, "Now the Lord said to Abram, 'Go forth from your country, and from your relatives, and from your father's house to the land which I will show you.' "[12]

Mere words cannot convey the searing totality of that call.   To leave all that is familiar and dear, and be wrenched from traditions long established, and to inflict pain upon loved ones by so sharp a severance and separation *is only the beginning*!   In the three-fold bond of country, kindred and father's house, God has put His finger upon all that can become fastened to the heart, mind and loyalty of men; indeed, all that constitutes a man's life.   Yet, if we will not hearken to that voice and depart, what real place can God have in us?   How much would we prefer to remain where we are and try to accommodate God at the same time by being as religious as possible in our own 'Ur of the Chaldees'?

---

[11] Deuteronomy 6:5
[12] Genesis 12:1

The Judaisms that men create are always the religions of convenience. They are religions that allow men to put on an outward show for God and think they are sincerely observant, while their inner and real lives are lived at Ur, amidst comforts, values and worldly blandishments with which they cannot part! So it was for the rich young ruler in Jesus' time, and so is it for us. The wisdom of the world that knows neither God nor His ways complains that surely God is not so cruel as to require such sacrifice! It quotes the commandment to honor father and mother to prove God is reasonable, and to imply that God would have you accommodate flesh and blood over Himself. The Judaisms of the world have always preferred sentiment to truth, the good thing to the *best* thing, and expediency to what is right. It is these Judaisms that quickly earn the applause of men, whose purposes they serve.

If the first demand to go forth from one's country were not enough, we have next an invitation to a radical, on-going walk with God: *to the land which I will show you.* It is a call to be guided through a wilderness into the land of promise; we must trust Him for every provision while the taunts ring in our ears for our foolishness at leaving everything—even 'betraying' our father's house and kin! Such is God's call to every man, and only those who, like Abraham, have heeded and obeyed, and who can now be made a blessing to all the families of the earth! Only unto those, as unto Abraham, does the Lord appear, making Himself manifest and real and thus enabling them to worship God truly.

"So he built an altar there to the Lord who had appeared to him...and called upon the name of the Lord."[13] How destitute is the world of real worship! How dry and mechanical are the forms we substitute for it! How demeaned we are by this failure, lost to pettiness, consigned to the ignoble, without the light of holiness,

---

[13] Ibid., vv. 7b, 8f

without joy—dead! Such is the fate of men to whom the living God has not appeared because they chose not to hear His voice, which called them to a continued going. "Abram journeyed on, *continuing* toward the Negev."[14]

---

[14] Ibid., v. 9

CHAPTER 3

THE JUDAISM OF JESUS

But at these words he [the rich young ruler] was saddened, and he went away grieving, for he was one who owned much property. And Jesus, looking around, said to His disciples, "How hard it will be for those who are wealthy to enter the kingdom of God!"

The disciples were amazed at His words. But Jesus answered again and said to them, "Children, how hard it is to enter the kingdom of God! It is easier for a camel to go through the eye of a needle than for a rich man to enter the kingdom of God."

They were even more astonished and said to Him, "Then who can be saved?"

Looking at them, Jesus said, "With people it is impossible, but not with God; for all things are possible with God."

Peter began to say to Him, "Behold, we have left everything and followed You."

Jesus said, "Truly I say to you, there is no one who has left house or brothers or sisters or mother or father or children or farms, for My sake and for the gospel's sake, but that he will receive a hundred times as much now in the present age, houses and brothers and sisters and mothers and children and farms, along with persecutions; and in the age to come, eternal life. But many who are first will be last, and the last, first."[1]

"Who then can be saved?"[2] asked the disciples of Jesus. They had just watched the encounter of this impressive, young Jewish man with Jesus and they had seen him mournfully turn away at Jesus' challenging word. They had no doubt that the matter was one of eternal salvation. The word *salvation* was a biblical term they were familiar with, unlike most of my modern Jewish kinsmen today who wince at the hearing of it, thinking it the invention of crude Christian fundamentalists!

"Come, follow Me," was Jesus' concluding word to the rich young man. In substance, it was the same challenge that God Himself had given to Abraham. How Jesus could give a command that was equal to God's invitation to Abraham, I leave the reader to ponder. Jesus acknowledged that the disciples had raised a legitimate point, namely, that the rejection of this call constituted the rejection of salvation.

It is rare to hear the word *salvation* from pulpits and platforms of today, be they Jewish or Gentile. Yet, the scriptures abound in references to the salvation that belongs to the Lord,[3] rejoicing in your salvation,[4] being saved with an everlasting salvation,[5] and the curse that is the consequence of not seeking for God's salvation: "And a fire was kindled against Jacob and anger also mounted

---

[1] Mark 10:22-31
[2] Ibid., v. 26
[3] Psalms 3:8
[4] Psalms 9:14
[5] Isaiah 45:17

against Israel, because they did not believe in God, and did not trust in His salvation."[6]

It is interesting how the rejection of God's salvation is equated in Scripture with the rejection of God:

> Now consider this, you who forget God, or I will tear you in pieces, and there will be none to deliver.   He who offers a sacrifice of thanksgiving honors Me; and to him who orders his way aright I shall show the salvation of God.[7]

These fierce verses are significant because they are addressed to the outwardly religious who lightly regard God's words, and they serve as a kind of survey of what we have endeavored to express until now. Let us seriously ponder the verses that go before this:

> But to the wicked God says, "What right have you to tell of My statutes and to take My covenant in your mouth?   For you hate discipline, and you cast My words behind you. When you see a thief, you are pleased with him, and you associate with adulterers. You let your mouth loose in evil and your tongue frames deceit. You sit and speak against your brother; you slander your own mother's son. These things you have done and I kept silence; you thought that I was just like you; I will reprove you and state the case in order before your eyes. Now consider this, you who forget God...[8]

What a contrast is offered to us in the psalm that follows! Psalms 51 is a psalm of penitence, and it clearly illustrates that which makes for salvation, that which is required from man, and that which God gives to us freely.

---

[6] Psalms 78:21b-22
[7] Psalms 50:22-23
[8] Psalms 50:16-22a

Here is essential biblical Judaism, expressed and set forth for those willing to order their conduct aright:

> Be gracious to me, O God, according to Your lovingkindness; according to the greatness of Your compassion blot out my transgressions. Wash me thoroughly from my iniquity and cleanse me from my sin. For I know my transgressions, and my sin is ever before me. Against You, You only, I have sinned and done what is evil in Your sight, so that You are justified when You speak and blameless when You judge.
>
> Behold, I was brought forth in iniquity, and in sin my mother conceived me. Behold, You desire truth in the innermost being, and in the hidden part You will make me know wisdom. Purify me with hyssop, and I shall be clean; wash me, and I shall be whiter than snow. Make me to hear joy and gladness, let the bones which You have broken rejoice. Hide Your face from my sins and blot out all my iniquities.
>
> Create in me a clean heart, O God, and renew a steadfast spirit within me. Do not cast me away from Your presence and do not take Your Holy Spirit from me. Restore to me the joy of Your salvation and sustain me with a willing spirit.[9]

Note the utter centrality of God in this psalm. It is *God's* mercy to which David appeals. God is the One sinned against; He alone is able to blot out our transgressions and wash us thoroughly from iniquity. He alone is Judge. His standard is higher, going beyond the minimal response of men and into the concealed places, to that which is not seen—the innermost being. He is the Creative God who is able to bestow a clean heart and a right spirit, to impart a wisdom that is not humanly

---

[9] Psalms 51: 1-12

attainable. The sum of all these things, not easily spoken of, but available to our experience, constitutes *salvation*! The evidence of a person's salvation is the possession of joy and the continual awareness of being sustained and upheld by the Spirit of God. To such a one, God's presence is sensed and real; God's indwelling Spirit is indeed the very light of his life.

Note also the utter dependence of man on God. Man's only part is to appeal and to repentantly acknowledge his transgressions and sins. Then salvation comes as a gift. There is nothing that man can do to effect his own salvation, but bring to God a broken spirit and a broken and contrite heart as being his sole hope, "The sacrifices of God are a broken spirit; a broken and contrite heart, O God, You will not despise."[10] This posture will not delight the hearts of proud men. On the contrary, God's salvation comes as a gift to the humbled and repentant. Salvation is a rank offense that grates against every stubborn impulse of conceit and self-justification that is in proud mankind. Such will rush to embrace those religions of the world that will provide them with the needed psychological, emotional and social benefits, and yet not require that a person be abased and that they humble themselves before the mighty hand of God. Proud mankind will prefer to endow synagogues and churches, buy bonds and support philanthropies—receiving, of course, appropriate public recognition—identify with causes, thinking of their activity as pleasing in God's sight. Such are repelled by the word *conversion* and look with great abhorrence upon any that should dare to speak of it to them. Yet the psalmist continues: "Then I will teach transgressors Your ways, and sinners will be converted to You."[11]

Here again we see a vital difference between the Judaism of God and the Judaism of men: one impels men to

---

[10] Ibid., v. 17
[11] Ibid., v. 13

"Cry loudly, do not hold back; raise your voice like a trumpet, and declare to My people their transgression and to the house of Jacob their sins."[12] The other professes concern for the sensibilities of men, prefers silence and decorum, looking upon the messenger of salvation as a troublemaker and offender of propriety and good taste. It becomes increasingly easy to detect the Judaism by which men actually live their lives independent of the professions they make. He who knows the salvation of God speaks out, while the others are invariably silent. In an age in which we are dying within and without, when the sanctifying and uplifting presence of God alone can save us from a deadening, mundane life, who is telling men about God? Hear the cry of the psalmist:

> Deliver me from bloodguiltiness, O God, the God of my salvation; then my tongue will joyfully sing of Your righteousness. O Lord, open my lips, that my mouth may declare Your praise.[13]

It is interesting that in all of the long debate about who or what a Jew is, no one seems to have considered that *Judah*, the Hebrew root from which the word *Jew* is derived, means *praise*! Can it be that a true Jew is one who can truly praise God? It follows then that the true Judaism of God must necessarily eventuate in the praise of God from the lips of men and women whom He alone has brought into His salvation [i.e., redeemed]. The rich young ruler, sorrowfully unable and unwilling to wholly commit himself to God, left Jesus in silence. In contrast, we will be examining an encounter with Jesus by a blind man whose response was totally the opposite.

---

[12] Isaiah 58:1
[13] Psalms 51:14-15

CHAPTER 4

JESUS, SON OF DAVID

As Jesus was approaching Jericho, a blind man was sitting by the road begging. Now hearing a crowd going by, he began to inquire what this was. They told him that Jesus of Nazareth was passing by. And he called out, saying, "Jesus, Son of David, have mercy on me!"

Those who led the way were sternly telling him to be quiet; but he kept crying out all the more, "Son of David, have mercy on me!"

And Jesus stopped and commanded that he be brought to Him; and when he came near, He questioned him, "What do you want Me to do for you?"

And he said, "Lord, I want to regain my sight!"

And Jesus said to him, "Receive your sight; your faith has made you well."

Immediately he regained his sight and began following Him, glorifying God; and when all the people saw it, they gave praise to God.[1]

---

[1] Luke 18:35-43

How suggestive it is that the rich young ruler, proud of his own conduct and asking what he must do to inherit eternal life, began by addressing Jesus as 'Good' Teacher. This failure to correctly identify Jesus made inevitable the spiritual failure of the interview that was to follow. Yet, in the account above, the blind beggar, hearing that Jesus was passing by cried out, "Jesus, Son of David."[2] He identified Jesus by His Messianic title, and thereby ended up receiving the mercy he asked for.

Then as now, identifying Jesus as Messiah is *everything*. He was a Master and teacher, but these titles are woefully incomplete; they would not have any saving power. Jesus said to the blind man, "Your faith has made you well."[3] We have already spoken of one of the distinctive qualities of God's Judaism—that it entails a measure of faith that is more than mere intellectual assent to correct doctrine, or a vague acknowledgment of the existence of some 'Higher Power.' True faith results in life-transforming power, because it casts itself upon the character of God and His word, and expects the fulfillment of what God has promised.

When Jesus heard the blind man's cry, He called for him, and "throwing aside his cloak, he jumped up and came to Jesus."[4] We cannot even begin to plumb the depths of this statement. No doubt it is both historical and symbolic. One can sense the shucking off of one's garment, no matter how threadbare, as an act of separation, of putting aside all that pertains to one's past life in order to rise and come into the promise of some barely apprehended 'newness.' For us, it would mean the garments of pride and accomplishment, and indeed every vain device of posturing and deceit that covers our nakedness. Be assured that until we shuck off those garments, however richly embroidered

---

[2] Ibid., v. 35
[3] Ibid., v. 42b
[4] Mark 10:50

and esteemed we may be in the world, in God's sight, "all of us have become like one who is unclean, and all our righteous deeds are like a filthy garment."[5] Only then can we say, "For You have hidden Your face from us and have delivered us into the power of our iniquities. But now, O LORD, You are our Father, we are the clay, and You our potter; and all of us are the work of Your hand."[6]

What then is the significance in identifying Jesus as the *Son of David*? Interestingly, the book of Matthew begins with: "The record of the genealogy of Jesus the Messiah, the son of David, the son of Abraham."[7] Although we Jews repeatedly acknowledge that Jesus was a Jew, the full impact of that fact has never seemed to register upon us. Perhaps we have seen too many depictions of a blue-eyed, Anglo-Saxon Christ, and in our minds, we associate Him with icons, incense and other alien paraphernalia of the religions of the Gentiles. Ironically, the majority of *Gentiles* seem to have never really recognized Jesus as a Jew! However tragic and unfortunate that is, something more than mere Jewish identity is meant by the title "Son of David." This title was well known to every Jew of Jesus' generation, who valued and pondered the scriptures, and who therefore knew it as the title of the promised Messiah!

Even the word *Messiah* has largely lost its meaning to most Jews, and is treated with the same airy neglect and vagueness as they treat God Himself. In the hearing of the word, some think mistily of a future but distant event by which peace will come to blanket the world—a kind of *messianic* age. Even fewer believe that that event will be brought about by a person, let alone a divine personage. Others would be disposed to believe the messianic age to be one of progress and reconciliation brought about by

---

[5] Isaiah 64:6a
[6] Isaiah 64:8-9
[7] Matthew 1:1

unaided human effort. For the blind beggar, for the disciples and the many who came to believe on Him, Jesus was the fulfillment of messianic prophecy that foretold the advent of a person who, among other attributes, would be of the lineage of David.

Unlike most modern men who go a whole lifetime without ever examining a Bible, the contemporaries of Jesus had a high regard for, and a greater familiarity with the scriptures. Most of them would have known, for instance, of the covenant God made with David:

> "When your days are fulfilled that you must go to be with your fathers, that I will set up one of your descendants after you, who will be of your sons; and I will establish his kingdom. He shall build for Me a house, and I will establish his throne forever. I will be his father and he shall be My son; and I will not take My lovingkindness away from him, as I took it from him who was before you. But I will settle him in My house and in My kingdom forever, and his throne shall be established forever."
>
> According to all these words and according to all this vision, so Nathan spoke to David.[8]

That a Messiah-King would come forth from the lineage of David was also established through the prophet Isaiah, who, by the divine inspiration of the Spirit of God, described the Messianic Kingdom that would be established when:

> ...the wolf will dwell with the lamb, and the leopard will lie down with the young goat, and the calf and the young lion and the fatling together; and a little boy will lead them. Also the cow and the bear will graze; their young will lie down together; and the lion will eat straw like

---

[8] 1 Chronicles 17:11-15

the ox. The nursing child will play by the hole
of the cobra, and the weaned child will put his
hand on the viper's den. They will not hurt or
destroy in all My holy mountain, for the earth
will be full of the knowledge of the Lord as the
waters cover the sea.

Then in that day the nations will resort to the
root of Jesse, who will stand as a signal for the
peoples; and His resting place will be glorious.[9]

It is evident that the "root of Jesse"[10] refers to a person
born out of that line. This is again reinforced in the
beginning verses of this same magnificent eleventh chapter:

Then a shoot will spring from the stem of Jesse,
and a branch from his roots will bear fruit. The
Spirit of the Lord will rest on Him, the spirit of
wisdom and understanding, the spirit of counsel
and strength, the spirit of knowledge and the fear
of the Lord.

And He will delight in the fear of the Lord, and
He will not judge by what His eyes see, nor
make a decision by what His ears hear; but with
righteousness He will judge the poor, and decide
with fairness for the afflicted of the earth; and
He will strike the earth with the rod of His
mouth, and with the breath of His lips He will
slay the wicked. Also righteousness will be the
belt about His loins, and faithfulness the belt
about His waist.[11]

Again, a *person* from the city of David, Bethlehem,
was expected to be the Messiah-King. Even non-Jews who
were familiar with the sacred, prophetic passages revered
Israel's God and knew about these messianic prophecies.

---

[9] Isaiah 11: 6-10

[10] Jesse was David's father

[11] Ibid., vv. 1-5

Concerning the fulfillment of these prophecies, Matthew writes:

> Now after Jesus was born in Bethlehem of Judea in the days of Herod the king, magi from the east arrived in Jerusalem, saying, "Where is He who has been born King of the Jews? For we saw His star in the east and have come to worship Him."[12]

As important it is to ponder why anyone outside of Jewish ethnicity would want to worship a king of the Jews, note, for now, the reaction of a jealous King Herod:

> When Herod the king heard this, he was troubled, and all Jerusalem with him. Gathering together all the chief priests and scribes of the people, he inquired of them where the Messiah was to be born. They said to him, "In Bethlehem of Judea, for so it has been written by the prophet: 'And you, Bethlehem, land of Judah, are by no means least among the leaders of Judah; for out of you shall come forth a ruler who will shepherd My people Israel.' "[13]

The well-known messianic prophecy to which they were alluding—of which today's non-biblical Jews are ignorant—was written eight centuries *before* the coming of the Messiah:

> But as for you, Bethlehem Ephrathah, too little to be among the clans of Judah, from you One will go forth for Me to be ruler in Israel. His goings forth are from long ago, from the days of eternity.[14]

It is in perfect keeping with a God whose thoughts are not our thoughts, and whose ways are not our ways, that the

---

[12] Matthew 2:1-2

[13] Ibid., vv. 3-6

[14] Micah 5:2

ruler of Israel should come from one of the least significant towns of Judah. This is the God who loves meekness and chooses the foolish things of the world to shame the wise.[15]

Therefore, any messianic expectancy of One who would come in pomp and glory, and that regarded the traditions of men over the prophetic word of God, was doomed to result in error. Only the *things that are written* can be the clear and sure guide. As we shall be examining later, the failure to omit any portion of the messianic portrait is as fatal as the rejection of all Scripture. We must come to the place of believing that "man does not live by bread alone, but man lives by everything that proceeds out of the mouth of the Lord."[16]   There are even more references to Old Testament messianic prophecy in the first few chapters of the gospel of Matthew:

> Now all this took place to fulfill what was spoken by the Lord through the prophet: "Behold, the virgin shall be with child and shall bear a Son, and they shall call His name Immanuel, which translated means, 'God with us' "[17] [referring to Isaiah 7:14].

> So Joseph got up and took the Child and His mother while it was still night, and left for Egypt. He remained there until the death of Herod. This was to fulfill what had been spoken by the Lord through the prophet: "Out of Egypt I called My Son"[18] [referring to Hosea 11:1].

The Judaism of Jesus is the Judaism of the prophetic scriptures which teach that God, by His Spirit, foretold the details of the coming Messiah centuries in advance. The scriptures also teach that He is faithful to fulfill them. In His every utterance and deed, Jesus exemplified *this*

---

[15] See 1 Corinthians 1:27-29

[16] Deuteronomy 8:3b

[17] Matthew 1:22-23

[18] Matthew 2:14-15

Judaism! He Himself believed that He was the fulfillment of messianic prophecy, affirming this again and again. With regards to the scriptures, it was He who said, "Do not think that I came to abolish the Law or the Prophets; I did not come to abolish, but to fulfill."[19]

---

[19] Matthew 5:17

CHAPTER 5

JESUS, THE ANOINTED ONE

"I give you my word of honor," is one of the phrases I treasure the most from my childhood. In that generation, a person's character was his most important possession. Solemn pacts were sealed by a word alone, and that word was only as solid and negotiable as the character of him who spoke it. Back then, a man's worth was measured by his integrity.

In our present day, one seldom hears such a phrase. TV culture and our consumer-oriented civilization have all conspired in this age to manipulate and corrupt the meanings of words. Indeed, flight from verbalization and rationality characterizes our generation, and has given way increasingly to an emphasis on impulse and feelings. Words have less value as we become inured to extravagant appeals for consumer products or by the empty promises of our political candidates. As a result, character has declined in like proportion to the weightlessness of much of our speech and utterances.

In stark contrast, few have spoken of the value of words themselves more penetratingly than Jesus. The most careful reader will not detect anything in His statements but the most measured utterances—always wholly consonant with His impeccable character and blameless existence. In fact, Jesus constantly reiterated the connection between what a man is and what He speaks, as in this portion from the account of Matthew, in which He addresses His critics, the Pharisees:

> You brood of vipers, how can you, being evil, speak what is good? For the mouth speaks out of that which fills the heart. The good man brings out of his good treasure what is good; and the evil man brings out of his evil treasure what is evil.[1]

Then, going far beyond the authority of even those who profess to be spokesmen for God, He added:

> But I tell you that every careless word that people speak, they shall give an accounting for it in the day of judgment. For by your words you will be justified, and by your words you will be condemned.[2]

If He could make such a radical statement about words, how much more, then, would we need to give our attention to *all* that He spoke? In my first encounter with His spoken Word, my own life was arrested and turned from atheistic indifference to the pursuit of God. His words were too radical to be ignored, and too unequivocal to be dismissed. Let us not be found satisfying ourselves with ignorant hearsay of what He spoke. His first words, with which He began His public ministry, thoroughly astounded those who heard them, and they have the same affect now. Let us endeavor to free ourselves from every misconception and common prejudice, so that we can enter into the dramatic and profound moment recorded for us in the book of Luke:

---

[1] Matthew 12:34,35
[2] Ibid., vv. 36,37

> And He came to Nazareth, where He had been brought up; and as was His custom, He entered the synagogue on the Sabbath, and stood up to read. And the book of the prophet Isaiah was handed to Him. And He opened the book and found the place where it was written, "The Spirit of the Lord is upon Me, because He anointed Me to preach the gospel to the poor; He has sent Me to proclaim release to the captives, and recovery of sight to the blind, to set free those who are oppressed, to proclaim the favorable year of the Lord."[3]

This passage from Isaiah 61 would have been familiar to all who knew the messianic scriptures, heralding the advent of *Meshiach*, the Anointed One, the long-awaited deliverer of Israel!

> And He closed the book, gave it back to the attendant and sat down; and the eyes of all in the synagogue were fixed on Him. And He began to say to them, "Today this Scripture has been fulfilled in your hearing."[4]

There is yet another occasion where Jesus claims to be the Messiah, as given to us in a conversation He had with a Samaritan woman at the well where He had gone to sit down. She acknowledged Him first as a Jew and then as a prophet, but she had failed to see Him fully as the Son of God:

> The woman said to Him, "I know that Messiah is coming (He who is called Christ); when that One comes, He will declare all things to us." Jesus said to her, "I who speak to you am He."[5]

---

[3] Luke 4:16-19
[4] Ibid., vv. 20-21
[5] John 4:25-26

What do you say to such unequivocal claims, dear reader? Can He who cautioned men about the severity of idle words make idle claims Himself? As Jews who suppose ourselves to be spiritually superior to Samaritans, it is to our shame that we go on to read:

> ...many of the Samaritans believed in Him because of the word of the [Samaritan] woman...[and] many more believed because of His word; and they were saying to the woman, "It is no longer because of what you said that we believe, for we have heard for ourselves and know that this One is indeed the Savior of the world."[6]

When Jesus asked of Simon Peter, "But who do you say that I am?" he answered, "You are the Christ, the Son of the living God," Jesus said to him, "Blessed are you, Simon Barjona."[7] And blessed is *every* man who comes to this same recognition!

We can no longer continue to applaud such a Man as a great teacher, a prophet or even a sublime preacher; something infinitely more is required. No middle ground is afforded us; His repeated claims disallow it. We must either affirm with Peter, "You are the Christ," or condemn Him for unspeakable blasphemy!

> The high priest stood up and came forward and questioned Jesus, saying, "Do You not answer? What is it that these men are testifying against You?"
>
> But He kept silent and did not answer. Again the high priest was questioning Him, and saying to Him, "Are You the Christ, the Son of the Blessed One?"
>
> And Jesus said, "I am; and you shall see the Son

---

[6] John 4:39-42
[7] Matthew 16:15b-17a

of Man sitting at the right hand of power, and
coming with the clouds of heaven." Tearing his
clothes, the high priest said, "What further need
do we have of witnesses? You have heard the
blasphemy; how does it seem to you?" And they
all condemned Him to be deserving of death.[8]

A short time later, Pontius Pilate asked Him, "Are You
the King of the Jews?" And He answered Him, "It is as you
say."[9] Such a confession as this must discomfort every
person who values truth and his own integrity, as indeed, it
is calculated to do. We cannot continue to blithely dismiss
this Jesus with a few compliments about being merely an
outstanding Jew or a great teacher. His repeated assertions
demand either extreme hatred or extreme commitment. He
really is who He repeatedly said that He is, or He really
was a blasphemer worthy of death. If He is not the
Messiah, then how can we as Jews, with a God-given
calling as a nation of priests and a light unto the nations,
indifferently allow Him to be worshiped by deluded
Gentiles everywhere? Should we not take the pains to
inform them about this *deceiver*? Can our consciences
permit the adherence, loyalty and worship of millions to a
grotesque blasphemer? Should we not encourage them to
turn to our own makeshift Judaism, rather than allow them
to be comforted unto death by a lie? More crucially, are we
going to align ourselves with those who have condemned
Him, or with those who worship Him? Is there any other
ground?

Very early in His ministry, Jesus compelled men to a
decision about Himself. The book of Mark records a
typical episode:

When He had come back to Capernaum several
days afterward, it was heard that He was at
home. And many were gathered together, so

---

[8] Mark 14:60-64
[9] Mark 15:2

that there was no longer room, not even near the door; and He was speaking the word to them. And they came, bringing to Him a paralytic, carried by four men. Being unable to get to Him because of the crowd, they removed the roof above Him; and when they had dug an opening, they let down the pallet on which the paralytic was lying. And Jesus, seeing their faith, said to the paralytic, "Son, your sins are forgiven."

But some of the scribes were sitting there and reasoning in their hearts, "Why does this man speak that way? He is blaspheming; who can forgive sins but God alone?"[10]

Again, in the book of John, our Jewish predicament and perplexity is deepened by a miracle that Jesus performed on a man who was blind from his birth. It was performed on the Sabbath, which infuriated the religious Jews:

"This man is not from God, because He does not keep the Sabbath." But others were saying, "How can a man who is a sinner perform such signs?" And there was a division among them.[11]

Note that the choice of the Sabbath was, of course, intentional. Healing on the Sabbath never did violate God's ordinance; the only thing that was violated was the labyrinth of man-made laws and traditions that had grown up around God's ordinance. The Pharisees interrogated both the parents and the man who could now see, the latter speaking with such acute wisdom and keen common sense as to lay bare the whole issue of Jesus' identity:

So a second time they called the man who had been blind, and said to him, "Give glory to God; we know that this man is a sinner." He then

---

[10] Mark 2:1-7
[11] John 9:16b

answered, "Whether He is a sinner, I do not
know; one thing I do know, that though I was
blind, now I see."

So they said to him, "What did He do to you?
How did He open your eyes?" He answered
them, "I told you already and you did not listen;
why do you want to hear it again? You do not
want to become His disciples too, do you?"
They reviled him and said, "You are His
disciple, but we are disciples of Moses. We
know that God has spoken to Moses, but as for
this man, we do not know where He is from."

The man answered and said to them, "Well, here
is an amazing thing, that you do not know where
He is from, and yet He opened my eyes. We
know that God does not hear sinners; but if
anyone is God-fearing and does His will, He
hears him. Since the beginning of time it has
never been heard that anyone opened the eyes of
a person born blind. If this man were not from
God, He could do nothing."[12]

At this they cast him out of the synagogue after saying,
"You were born entirely in sins, and are you teaching
us?"[13] Jesus learned of this man's expulsion and finding
him, He asked him the question that continues to confound
Jewish theology:

"Do you believe in the Son of Man?" He
answered, "Who is He, Lord, that I may believe
in Him?" Jesus said to him, "You have both
seen Him, and He is the one who is talking with
you." And he said, "Lord, I believe." And he
worshiped Him.[14]

---

[12] John 9:24-33
[13] Ibid., v.34
[14] Ibid., vv. 35-38

CHAPTER 6

THE MYSTERY OF THE GODHEAD

Perhaps the single greatest difficulty in the Jewish consideration of Jesus is our adamant insistence on *one* God. Who is this who forgives men their sins, who allows Jews to worship Him and address Him as Lord, who speaks with an authority that exceeds every prophet that preceded Him, who performs miracles of unprecedented power, and who claims to be God's very Son? This supposed King of the Jews? Whatever our insistence that God has no son, whatever our assurance that God shares His deity with no one, that He would never come as a man, that one cannot be both Messiah and God, that the Messiah could not have come as yet because we have not yet world peace, and every other traditional Jewish objection, we are still confronted with a Jesus whose claims, deeds and character threaten to explode it all.

Again and again, Jesus perplexed His Jewish contemporaries by His continual references to His Father: He told them He was sent of His Father (John 8:42), that the words He spoke were from His Father (John 8:26), that He came to do the will of His Father (John 6:38), that to have seen Him is to have seen the Father (John 14:9), that

He goes to the Father (John 16:17), and that the Father is with Him (John 16:32).

The book of John is almost one continual chronicle of these startling encounters, in which Jesus affirms His deity and equality with the Father to the astounded Jewish audience, and as always, "A division occurred again among the Jews because of these words."[1] In one single conversation, Jesus said of Himself,

> I am the door; if anyone enters through Me, he will be saved, and will go in and out and find pasture. The thief comes only to steal and kill and destroy; I came that they may have life, and have it abundantly.
>
> I am the good shepherd; the good shepherd lays down His life for the sheep...I am the good shepherd, and I know My own and My own know Me.[2]

In the Old Testament, God describes *Himself* as the Shepherd: "...Behold, I Myself will search for My sheep and seek them out."[3] Yet, He says, "My servant David...will feed them himself and be their shepherd."[4] These references to being the Shepherd of Israel would identify Jesus as the fulfillment of the covenant that God prophesied about in Ezekiel, the Shepherd-Lord of Psalm 23. Jesus' hearers were informed about these passages, and understandably perplexed because we read that they "gathered around Him," and asked,

> "How long will You keep us in suspense? If You are the Christ, tell us plainly." Jesus answered them, "I told you, and you do not believe; the works that I do in My Father's name, these testify of Me...My sheep hear My

---

[1] John 10:19
[2] John 10:9-11,14
[3] Ezek. 34:11b
[4] Ibid., v. 23

> voice...and I give eternal life to them, and they
> will never perish...My Father, who has given
> them to Me, is greater than all; and no one is
> able to snatch them out of the Father's hand. I
> and the Father are one." The Jews took up
> stones again to stone Him.[5]

Once again, as Jews, we are left with the perplexing
and painful choice between the unprecedented claims of
Jesus versus all that we have understood to be true about
the Messiah. The logic of their position demanded death
for a blasphemer; we are not exempt from the same
difficult choice these many centuries later. As long as
these words continue to reverberate through time, we are
invited to follow the Good Shepherd, or else take up stones
to stone Him! The unwillingness to seriously consider His
claims is the same as taking up stones to stone Him; albeit
the stones of indifference and rejection.

> Jesus answered them, "I showed you many good
> works from the Father; for which of them are
> you stoning Me?" The Jews answered Him,
> "For a good work we do not stone You, but for
> blasphemy; and because You, being a man,
> make Yourself out to be God."[6]

Did not God, speaking through the prophet Micah,
exclaim that He who was to come forth from Bethlehem to
be Ruler (King) in Israel was also the One whose "goings
forth are from long ago, from the days of eternity"?[7] We
were also foretold that,

> For a child will be born to us, a son will be given
> to us; and the government will rest on His
> shoulders; and His name will be called Wonder-
> ful Counselor, Mighty God, Eternal Father,
> Prince of Peace.

---

[5] John 10:24-31
[6] Ibid., vv.32,33
[7] Micah 5:2f

> There will be no end to the increase of His
> government or of peace, on the throne of David
> and over His kingdom, to establish it and to
> uphold it with justice and righteousness from
> then on and forevermore. The zeal of the Lord
> of hosts will accomplish this.[8]

We should have fastened upon the scriptures that
assured us, "Behold, the Lord God will come with might,
with His arm ruling for Him...Like a shepherd He will tend
His flock"[9] and "Do not fear, you worm Jacob, you men of
Israel; I will help you," declares the Lord, "and your
Redeemer is the Holy One of Israel."[10] In one of the
clearest Old Testament references to the mystery of the
Triune God, we read:

> Behold, My Servant, whom I uphold; My
> chosen one in whom My soul delights. I have
> put My Spirit upon Him; He will bring forth
> justice to the nations...He will not be
> disheartened or crushed until He has established
> justice in the earth; and the coastlands will wait
> expectantly for His law. Thus says God the
> Lord, who created the heavens and stretched
> them out, who spread out the earth and its
> offspring, who gives breath to the people on it
> and spirit to those who walk in it, "I am the
> Lord, I have called you in righteousness, I will
> also hold You by the hand and watch over You,
> and I will appoint You as a covenant to the
> people, as a light to the nations, to open blind
> eyes, to bring out prisoners from the dungeon,
> and those who dwell in darkness from the
> prison.[11]

---

[8] Isaiah 9:6-7
[9] Isaiah 40:10,11
[10] Isaiah 41:14
[11] Isaiah 42:1-7

Of whom is God speaking? Who is this *Servant* up whom His Spirit is, who will be a *light to the nations* a One to open blind eyes? The mystery is compounded the following verses from Isaiah:

> Thus says the Lord, the King of Israel and his Redeemer, the Lord of Hosts: "I am the first and I am the last, and there is no God besides Me" (44:6);
>
> Thus says the Lord, the Holy One of Israel, and his Maker (45:11);
>
> Thus says the Lord, the Redeemer of Israel and its Holy One, to the despised One, to the One abhorred by the nation (49:7);
>
> From the first I have not spoken in secret, from the time it took place, I was there. And now the Lord God has sent Me, and His Spirit (48:16).

These verses give every impression of an *Elohim* who is a compound unity of persons and is yet One! Can it be that the reference to God the Creator in the first chapter of Genesis, "Let *us* make man in *our* image" is not a grammatical flourish of majesty, but a reference from the beginning of this composite unity? In the famous verse, "Shema Yisroel adonoi elohenu adonoi echod" (Hear, O Israel, the Lord our God is one Lord), *echod* means one in unity, unlike *ached*, which means singular one. Instead of being used as a bulwark against the claims of Jesus, this verse was intended to be the very grounds for our acceptance of Him.

The biblical Judaism of God affirms just these things:

> In the beginning was the Word, *and the Word was with God, and the Word was God*...All things came into being through Him, and apart from Him nothing came into being that has come into being. In Him was life, and the life was the light of men...the true light which, coming into the world, enlightens every man. He was in the world, and the world was made

through Him, and the world did not know Him...*And the Word became flesh, and dwelt among us*, and we saw His glory, glory as of the only begotten from the Father, full of grace and truth.[12]

How ironic that God, being made manifest in the flesh, being born as a Son, appears to us as *Christian* doctrine, completely alien to Jewish thought, when all of these statements are clearly set forth in our own Hebrew scriptures! One might even imagine that our spiritual leaders have taken pains to keep us from this biblical understanding for fear that we might find uncomfortable *Christological* implications in them. To our shame, we seem to be more familiar with Jewish traditions that repudiate the claims of Jesus as the Messiah—which seems to be a continuation of the same issues that Jesus Himself addressed nearly two thousand years ago:

"But in vain do they worship Me, teaching as doctrines the precepts of men. *Neglecting the commandment of God*, you hold to the tradition of men...You are experts at setting aside the commandment of God in order to keep your tradition...*invalidating the word of God by your tradition* which you have handed down; and you do many such things such as that."[13]

Jesus admonished His listeners, "You search the scriptures because you think that in them you have eternal life; it is these that testify about Me."[14] He was, of course, referring to the Old Testament, or Hebrew scriptures, for there were no other at that time. "For if you believed Moses, you would believe Me, for he wrote about Me."[15] Unhappily, very few modern Jews know what Moses and

---

[12] John 1:1-14. Emphases mine
[13] Mark 7:7-13. Emphases mine
[14] John 5:39
[15] John 5:46

the prophets wrote. Though we are an extremely literate people, yet are we biblical illiterates, lacking even the most rudimentary grasp of the scriptures. God's lament is:

> And when they say to you, "...Should not a people consult their God...To the law and to the testimony! If they do not speak according to this word, it is because they have no dawn."[16]

We invite you, dear reader, to put aside every presupposition, and to remember that nothing is impossible with God, whose "ways are not our ways, or His thoughts our thoughts." Earnestly ponder the scriptures that are cited throughout these pages, "For they are life to those who find them and health to all their body."[17]

---

[16] Isaiah 8:19-20
[17] Proverbs 4:22

CHAPTER 7

THE ONLY BEGOTTEN OF THE FATHER

In our general biblical ignorance, we Jews are adamant that God has *no* Son! Yet, as we have already seen, the Jews of Jesus' generation, far more familiar with the scriptures than we, anticipated a Messiah-King who would be born in Bethlehem, and who would be the Son of David. That He was also the Son of God was made known by Jesus to the religious leaders who apprehended and interrogated Him prior to His suffering and death:

> And the high priest said to Him, "I adjure You by the living God, that You tell us whether You are the Christ, *the Son of God*." Jesus said to him, "You have said it yourself; nevertheless I tell you, hereafter you will see the Son of Man sitting at the right hand of power, and coming on the clouds of heaven." Then the high priest tore his robes and said, "He has blasphemed! What further need do we have of witnesses? Behold, you have now heard the blasphemy; what do you think?" They answered, "He deserves death!"[1]

---

[1] Matthew 26:63-66

Unlike us, they had undoubtedly pondered the Messianic prophecies many times, trying to piece together the portrait of the promised Messiah that is given there. There are many profound clues scattered throughout Isaiah's writings, waiting to be revealed, but only to those who truly pant after God's fulfillment, who search the scriptures, and who, putting aside their own human notions, have eyes and a disposition of heart to see. Consider, for example, this portion of Scripture:

> Listen to Me, O islands, and pay attention, you peoples from afar. The Lord called Me from the womb; from the body of My mother He named Me. He has made My mouth like a sharp sword, in the shadow of His hand He has concealed Me; and He has also made Me a select arrow, He has hidden Me in His quiver...

> And now says the Lord, who formed Me from the womb to be His Servant, to bring Jacob back to Him, so that Israel might be gathered to Him (for I am honored in the sight of the Lord, and My God is My strength), He says, "It is too small a thing that You should be My Servant to raise up the tribes of Jacob and to restore the preserved ones of Israel; I will also make You a light of the nations so that My salvation may reach to the end of the earth.[2]

Add this to what we saw earlier in Isaiah, "For *a child will be* born to us, *a son will be given* to us; and the government will rest on His shoulders; and His name will be called Wonderful Counselor, Mighty God, Eternal Father, Prince of Peace,"[3] which adds to the clue given in an earlier verse: "Therefore the Lord Himself will give you a sign: Behold, a virgin will be with child and *bear a son*,

---

[2] Isaiah 49:1-6
[3] Isaiah 9:6. Emphases mine

and she will call His name Immanuel [God with us],"[4] and then consider the New Testament account which simply puts forth the factual fulfillment.

> Now the birth of Jesus Christ was as follows: when His mother Mary had been betrothed to Joseph, *before they came together* she was found to be with child by the Holy Spirit. And Joseph her husband, being a righteous man and not wanting to disgrace her, planned to send her away secretly.   But when he had considered this, behold, an angel of the Lord appeared to him in a dream, saying, "Joseph, son of David, do not be afraid to take Mary as your wife; for *the Child who has been conceived in her is of the Holy Spirit*. She will bear a Son; and you shall call His name Jesus, for He will save His people from their sins." *Now all this took place to fulfill what was spoken by the Lord through the prophet:* "Behold, the virgin shall be with child and shall bear a Son, and they shall call His name Immanuel," which translated means, "God with us."[5]

You may protest, "I cannot believe the New Testament," but why should it be any less believable than the Book that precedes it, having the same Author? "But it is not *our* Book," you may continue. Why is it *not* yours, if it is "able to make you wise unto salvation"? Did *your* Book make you wise unto salvation?   O, to be a Jew who is one inwardly! Concerning this inward kind of Judaism, the Jewish apostle Paul writes,

> For he is not a Jew who is one outwardly, nor is circumcision that which is outward in the flesh. But he is a Jew who is one inwardly; and circumcision is that which is of the heart, by the

---

[4] Isaiah 7:14. Emphasis mine
[5] Matthew 1:18-23. Emphases mine

> Spirit, not by the letter; and his praise is not
> from men, but from God.[6]

We cannot have it both ways; our God is not a God of compromise and accommodation. We must choose either the Judaism of men or the Judaism of God!

Little wonder the Holy Spirit cries out through the Psalmist,

> Why are the nations in an uproar and the peoples
> devising a vain thing? The kings of the earth
> take their stand, and the rulers take counsel
> together *against the Lord and against His
> Anointed*, saying, "Let us tear *their* fetters apart,
> and cast away *their* cords from us!" He who sits
> in the heavens laughs, the Lord scoffs at them.
> Then He will speak to them in His anger and
> terrify them in His fury, saying, "But as for Me,
> I have installed My King upon Zion, My holy
> mountain." I will surely tell of the decree of the
> Lord: He said to Me, *"Your are My Son, today I
> have begotten You. Ask of Me, I will surely
> give the nations as Your inheritance, and the
> very ends of the earth as Your possession."*[7]

Of whom do these scriptures speak? If we do not strain against their apparent meaning, then it is very clear. Is it possible that the calamities we have suffered through the centuries are but the fulfillment of the words, *the Lord scoffs at them*? Can our tragic history be interpreted as the judgment of a God who promises He *will speak to them in His anger and terrify them in His fury*? Let us consider the remainder of these scriptures:

> You shall break them with a rod of iron, You
> shall shatter them like earthenware. Now
> therefore, O kings, show discernment; take

---

[6] Romans 2:28-29
[7] Psalms 2:1-8. Emphases mine

warning, O judges of the earth. Worship the
Lord with reverence and rejoice with trembling.
Do homage to the Son, that He not become
angry, and you perish in the way, for His wrath
may soon be kindled. How blessed are all who
take refuge in Him![8]

The whole issue of these verses is centered on the *Son*.
It is unquestionably the issue of real religion as against that
which is only nominal; real service for God as against mere
verbal profession, real rejoicing—the result of a salvation
experience—as against lifeless religiosity; real fear and
trembling before an awesome God instead of cerebral
concepts of an indistinct *higher power*. How the world
delights in ambiguity about God! These vagaries and
generalizations are pleasing to the ear, but they cost
nothing, demand nothing and they obtain nothing. Not so
is the Judaism of our God, which requires that we *do
homage to the Son*, specifically acknowledge Him, draw
nigh to, submit to, honor and love Him, as is due the only
begotten from the Father. Anything less is to be *against
His Anointed*, and to be against His Anointed is to be *against the Lord*! Be wise, therefore, and "show discernment,
lest you perish in the way" is the sober admonition of a
God who says what He means and means what He says. In
this context, how meaningful are these sharp and repeated
utterances of Jesus: "...he who rejects Me rejects the One
who sent Me,"[9] and "...He who does not honor the Son
does not honor the Father who sent Him,"[10] and "And
blessed is he who does not take offense at Me."[11]

To be dogmatic about matters that are of eternal
consequence has somehow become an offense in the world,
which insists upon precision in every other area of life. For

---

[8] Ibid., vv. 9-12
[9] Luke 10:16f
[10] John 5:23b
[11] Matthew 11:6

those who would not tolerate guesswork from the mechanic who tunes their cars and certainly not from the pilot who lands their planes, may I advise the reader to have the same respect for specificity as is expressed in the following scriptures: "Whoever denies the Son does not have the Father; the one who confesses the Son has the Father also,"[12] and "Whoever believes that Jesus is the Christ is born of God, and whoever loves the Father loves the child born of Him,"[13] and "Anyone who goes too far and does not abide in the teaching of Christ, does not have God; the one who abides in the teaching, he has both the Father and the Son."[14] *Whoever* and *anyone* are not a haphazard choice of words, but the careful deliberation of a God who would that none be lost, but that *all* would come to Him. Whatever may be your subjective *feeling* about God, however assured you are that you know Him and love Him, *what do you believe about His Son?*

> For God so loved the world, that He gave *His only begotten Son*, that whoever believes in Him shall not perish, but have eternal life. For God did not send the Son into the world to judge the world, but that the world might be saved through Him. He who believes in Him is not judged; he who does not believe has been judged already, because he has not believed in the name of *the only begotten Son of God*.[15]

---

[12] 1 John 2:23
[13] 1 John 5:1
[14] 2 John 1:9
[15] John 3:16-18. Emphases mine

CHAPTER 8

CHRIST OUR PASSOVER

> The next day he [John the Baptist] saw Jesus
> coming to him and said, "Behold, the Lamb of
> God who takes away the sin of the world!"[1]

There is nothing as offensive to modern taste and
sensibility as the idea of sin. The word has an alien ring to
it, and quite out of keeping with our perception of the
underlying causes of human conduct. In our age of
psychological and sociological sophistication, one can
always call up an extenuating circumstance of biology or
environment to justify our behavior and obviate our
responsibility.

In a relativistic *milieu,* no standard can be established,
so that lying, stealing and cheating become common
practices in every community. The same practices,
magnified and extended, convulse the world, but they are
no different in kind from the white lies, indiscretions,
lapses and oversights that punctuate the daily experience of
most everyone.

---

[1] John 1:29

Our consciences are barely grieved, often lulled into a self-justifying limbo, aided by pills and various other synthetic devices of escape, which enable us to smother that still, small voice of conscience. Those who have a religious bent can attend their respective Jewish or Gentile temples for an hour or so of soothing organ peals, peaceful chanting and comforting allusions to the evils of society. Not many are exhorted to spiritually return to the base of the Holy Mount to hear the God of righteousness thunder from Sinai, "THOU SHALT NOT!"

Interestingly, the same God who specifically insists that we receive His Son is equally as specific in His definition of sin and His insistence that we take personal responsibility for it. One wonders if the rejection of His Son is a rejection of a specific standard of holiness that would seriously impinge upon our present, comfortable lifestyle. The problem of belief is not so much intellectual as it is moral; it is not so much a matter of being able to believe as it is being willing to accept everything concomitant to belief! The God of Abraham, who we thought was a God of convenience, might indeed actually be a consuming fire, and there are few who are anxious to find *that* kind of God. We maintain, and the scriptures maintain, that finding God is the primary purpose of being in this life, but this concept seems to have escaped the attention of the multitudes. Paul beautifully expressed this to a sophisticated audience of Greek pagans in Athens, and the modern pagan world would do well to heed these words:

> The God who made the world and all things in it, since He is Lord of heaven and earth, does not dwell in temples made with hands; nor is He served by human hands, as though He needed anything, since He Himself gives to all people life and breath and all things; and He made from one man every nation of mankind to live on all the face of the earth, having determined *their*

appointed times and the boundaries of their habitation, *that they would seek God*, if perhaps they might grope for Him *and find Him*, though He is not far from each one of us.[2]

How many Jewish inquirers, not to mention Gentile, would find their questions about Christ and the Bible answered by simply calling upon the God of Abraham, Isaac, and Jacob, and asking, "O God, if these things be true, if Jesus is your Son and the Messiah of Israel, if you would have me to follow Him, please reveal this to me and I will do so." Yet, it is amazing how few of us, even those who supposedly seek after truth, are willing to adopt so simple an expedient. Would we be fearful, perhaps, of receiving an answer? Jesus addressed this moral cowardice when He said,

> …My teaching is not Mine, but His who sent Me. If anyone is willing to do His will, he will know of the teaching, whether it is of God, or whether I speak from Myself.[3]

Are you prepared in your heart to *do His will*, and by implication, to suffer reproach on His behalf, be misunderstood, be seen as fanatic, alienate your best friends, risk your job and security, or lose your family? This is perhaps the deepest meaning and consequence of "loving the Lord your God with all your heart, all your soul, all your might...and having no other gods before Him." In our opinion, nothing more deeply and accurately reveals our true moral condition than our response to this Christ. What an acid test that God, in His wisdom, has flung in the face of both the religious and secular world with the sending of His Christ—the image of the invisible

---

[2] Acts 17:24-27. Emphases mine
[3] John 7:16-17

God[4] and the radiance of His glory and the exact representation of His nature.[5]

How we can profess to love God the Father and fail to recognize Him who is made in the Father's image is indeed a contradiction that is difficult to understand. How prophetic were the words of Simeon at the temple in Jerusalem, where Jesus' parents brought Him to present Him to the Lord, according to the Law:

> And there was a man in Jerusalem whose name was Simeon; and this man was righteous and devout, looking for the consolation of Israel; and the Holy Spirit was upon him. And it had been revealed to him by the Holy Spirit that he would not see death before he had seen the Lord's Christ. And he came in the Spirit into the temple; and when the parents brought in the child Jesus, to carry out for Him the custom of the Law, then he took Him into his arms, and blessed God, and said, "Now Lord, You are releasing Your bond-servant to depart in peace, according to Your word; for my eyes have seen Your salvation, which You have prepared in the presence of all peoples, a light of revelation to the Gentiles and the glory of Your people Israel"...And Simeon blessed them, and said to Mary His mother, "Behold, this Child is appointed for the fall and rise of many in Israel, and for a sign to be opposed—and a sword will pierce even your own soul—to the end *that thoughts from many hearts may be revealed.*"[6]

It is a temptation to linger over that remarkable portion of Scripture and comment on all that it so richly suggests. Let it suffice now to draw to your attention the kind of man

---

[4] Colossians 1:15
[5] Hebrews 1:3
[6] Luke 2:25-35. Emphasis mine

to whom God readily reveals His Christ. Simeon, we learned, was devout and righteous and *looking for the consolation of Israel*. Few have any appreciation of the fact that Israel is in need of being consoled by God. Fewer still are looking or waiting for it! Notice the remarkable ministry of the Spirit of God that was upon Simeon, and told him that he was not to die until he had seen that for which he was waiting and led him to the temple at the exact time Jesus was brought there.

Again, the reality of the Spirit of God in the life of the believer is the definitive aspect of the Judaism of God, as every believer can testify, Jew or Gentile. By this same Spirit, Simeon prophesied that Jesus was *appointed for the fall and rise of many in Israel, and for a sign to be opposed...that thoughts from many hearts may be revealed.* This has ever been the effect of the Word of God upon men, which is likely why we shrink from it, whether recorded in the scriptures, spoken by God's prophets, or made flesh to dwell among us! "For the word of God is living and active and sharper than any two-edged sword...and [it is] able to judge the thoughts and intentions of the heart."[7]

In the light of this, what then is our response to the Word of God who was made flesh? How strange that modern man is as unwilling to believe in God's judgment for sin as he is unwilling to believe in the concept of sin itself, and therefore, he despises God's redemption for it. These concepts are at the heart of the Judaism of God, but are repellant to the Judaisms of the world. Once again we are faced with the proposition of choosing between the Word of God as against all of the impelling and impressive things that weigh against it—the soothing assurances of the world that we are basically alright, that progress, or science, or the next generation will solve our ills, and not least, our own subjective feelings that we are not really *that*

---

[7] Hebrews 4:12

bad. The fact that few feel the need of God or feel the burden of their own iniquity is, perhaps, the most compelling evidence of the very cancer of sin itself. The words of Jesus echo still:

> It is not those who are healthy who need a physician, but those who are sick. But go and learn what this means, "I desire compassion, and not sacrifice, *for I did not come to call the righteous, but sinners.*"[8]

---

[8] Matthew 9:12-13. Emphasis mine

CHAPTER 9

REPENTANCE: THE KEY TO THE KINGDOM

If the things concerning Christ are true, how is it that so many clever men have missed it? Indeed, it is baffling how a people noted for intellectual acuity could have missed so apparent a message, both in Christ's own generation and then down through the ages to the present. The mystery is all the more compounded when considering the number of outstanding rabbis and scholars through the centuries who have given their lives to the painstaking examination of religious questions. Furthermore, it is baffling to learn that the chief adversaries of Jesus were often the religious leaders of the community, notably the Pharisees, who were the orthodox practitioners of Jesus' day. Jesus spoke most severely to them, and therefore, they were the ones most infuriated by Him. Consider this for example:

> Truly I say to you that the tax collectors and prostitutes will get into the kingdom of God before you. For John came to you in the way of righteousness and you did not believe him; but the tax collectors and prostitutes did believe

him; and you, seeing this, did not even feel remorse afterward so as to believe him.[1]

To say that the two most morally odious groups in Jewish society would enter the kingdom of God before these impeccably observant religious men was to add insult to injury. The point is that the tax collectors and prostitutes believed John the Baptist and were persuaded of the need to repent, to turn from their unrighteousness, and contritely return to God. Their belief eventuated in the act of water baptism. Baptism is a relinquishing of something, a giving up, a *mikvah* or symbolic purging in water, a turning to the living God in anticipation of Messiah for whom they have been prepared.

For all of the Pharisees' supposed righteousness, Jesus yet expected them to repent, even as the gross sinners who preceded them did, and, conversely their failure to repent disqualified them from believing! Here are some principles of the Judaism of God that we can deduce from Jesus' significant words, which are opposed to the principles of man-made Judaisms: Repentance is the voluntary and willing response of the individual toward God. If the most impeccably religious are in need of repentance, then all men everywhere should repent. Repentance is not waiting upon suitable feelings, but acting in compliance with God's wishes, having believed His Word. The refusal to repent precludes any possibility of believing. Believing, therefore, is not a matter of mind; it is a matter of heart.

"Watch over your heart with all diligence, for from it flows the springs of life."[2] This is not to suggest that we are to abandon the use of intellect in our inquiries toward God, but that the primary matter is integrity of heart, which opens to us the illuminations of the Spirit of God. Without revelation from the Spirit, the intellect is useless. Perhaps this will begin to explain how a blind beggar could see the

---

[1] Matthew 21:31,32
[2] Proverbs 4:23

Son of David in Jesus, while a rich young ruler who had kept all the commandments from his youth up could only see Him as a *good teacher*. Brilliance, leadership, esteem, learning and intellect are the factors that most encourage human pride and blind the arrogant to the sublime truth, which is evident only to the meek.

> Therefore, hear the word of the Lord, O scoffers, who rule this people who are in Jerusalem... Behold, I am laying in Zion a stone, a tested stone, a costly cornerstone for the foundation, firmly placed. He who believes in it will not be disturbed.[3]

> Then He shall become a sanctuary; but to both the houses of Israel, a stone to strike and a rock to stumble over, and a snare and a trap for the inhabitants of Jerusalem. Many will stumble over them, then they will fall and be broken; they will even be snared and caught.[4]

> The stone which the builders rejected has become the chief corner stone. This is the Lord's doing; it is marvelous in our eyes.[5]

How the same person can be for some a sanctuary, a precious stone, a foundation, and very salvation, and yet for others an object of scorn and rejection is the melancholy history of all that has attended that Rock, who is Christ. Pride is an abomination in God's sight. In order that "no man should boast before God," He chose the "...foolish things of the world to shame the wise, and God has chosen the weak things of the world to shame the things which are strong, and the base things of the world and the despised..."[6] Paul tells us that "a natural man does not accept the things of the Spirit of God; for they are

---

[3] Isaiah 28:14,16
[4] Isaiah 8:14-15
[5] Psalms 118:22
[6] 1 Corinthians 1:27-29

foolishness to him, and he cannot understand them, because they are spiritually appraised."[7]

In the last analysis, then, God must "show the salvation of God,"[8] which He does only to the seeking and repentant heart! In the final chapter of Isaiah, which begins with a "Thus says the Lord," we are told of the kind of man whom God will acknowledge: "But to this one I will look, to him who is humble and contrite of spirit, and who trembles at My word."[9] To tremble at His word is to believe that God is in earnest when He speaks of eternity, and that the Jesus who cautioned us about idle words, referred again and again to a hell "where their worm does not die, and the fire is not quenched."[10] He was confirming God's conclusion to the book of Isaiah:

> Then they will go forth and look on the corpses
> of the men who have transgressed against Me.
> For their worm will not die and their fire will not
> be quenched; and they will be an abhorrence to
> all mankind.[11]

In order to assure His audience of the utter seriousness of such a death, He repeats Himself twice in Luke: "...*unless you repent*, you will all likewise perish."[12] In Paul's dissertation to the Athenian intellectuals at Mars Hill, he assured them that God was:

> ...declaring to men that all people everywhere
> should repent, because He has fixed a day in
> which He will judge the world in righteousness
> through a Man whom He has appointed.[13]

---

[7] 1 Corinthians 2:14
[8] Psalms 50:23b
[9] Isaiah 66:2b
[10] Mark 9:43-48
[11] Isaiah 66:24
[12] Luke 13:3, 5. Emphasis mine
[13] Acts 17:30b-31a

This is no New Testament doctrine that is alien to Judaism. On the contrary, this is the very burden of biblical Judaism, as the whole thrust of the scriptures attest:

> How blessed is he whose transgression is forgiven, whose sin is covered! How blessed is the man to whom the Lord does not impute iniquity, and in whose spirit there is no deceit...I acknowledged my sin to You, and my iniquity I did not hide; I said, "I will confess my transgressions to the Lord"; and You forgave the guilt of my sin. Selah. Therefore, let everyone who is godly pray to You in a time when You may be found; surely in a flood of great waters they shall not reach him.[14]

Where shall repentance begin for one who feels no remorse but is persuaded by the scriptures that he ought? What better place to express remorse than over the scriptures themselves, in that we have ignored or rejected them, living by our own standards, and thus falling far short of the standard of God! "Behold, You desire truth in the innermost being."[15] We should have known, we who daily traffic in deceit and concealment. Let us repent for our lovelessness, our lack of real concern for others, our unwillingness to be inconvenienced, our utter self-centeredness, our shams, our pretense, our secret lusts and covetousness, our resentment and bitterness, our unforgiving spirits, our pride, and in the face of all these things, our neglect of God!

O, that we would have that vision of God "high and lifted up," in whose holy light we can see ourselves as we truly are. We would surely cry out like Isaiah when he glimpsed his own sinful state, "Woe is me, for I am ruined! Because I am a man of unclean lips, and I live among a

---

[14] Psalms 32:1-6
[15] Psalms 51:6

people of unclean lips; for my eyes have seen the King, the Lord of hosts."[16]

What, then, will *we* say when we stand before the King of glory? If one of the choicest prophets of God, Isaiah, could cry out in this way, what should be the response of lesser men who have lying and flattering lips? Surely the fear of God is no longer before our faces. Surely the world's spirit has deadened our awe of Him. What will we say when we see Him? Daniel only saw one of His angels and described the experience in the following passage: "…no strength was left in me, for my natural color turned to a deathly pallor, and I retained no strength…I fell into a deep sleep on my face, with my face to the ground."[17]

Even Job, who is described as "blameless, upright, fearing God and turning away from evil," acknowledges, "Behold, I am insignificant; what can I reply to You? I lay my hand on my mouth. Once I have spoken, and I will not answer; even twice, and I will add no more."[18] Later he says, "I have heard of You by the hearing of the ear; but now my eye sees You; therefore I retract, and I repent in dust and ashes."[19] Because of Job's right response, God tells him to pray for his three comforters, who are full of theological self-assurance: "For I will accept him so that I may not do with you according to your folly, *because you have not spoken of Me what is right, as My servant Job has.*"[20]

There is only one proper place for a man before the Holy God who does not change: "I retract, and I repent in dust and ashes." This is the same Lord who "restored the fortunes of Job,"[21] and who, hearing the contrite, broken

---

[16] Isaiah 6:5
[17] Daniel 10:8b-9
[18] Job 40:4-5
[19] Job 42:5-6
[20] Ibid., v. 8b. Emphasis mine
[21] Ibid., v. 10

cry of Isaiah, provided the live coal from His altar, to cleanse him: "He touched my mouth with it and said, 'Behold, this has touched your lips; and your iniquity is taken away and your sin is forgiven.' "[22] This same Lord has made provision, *as only He can*, to take iniquity away and purge all of our sins—if only we would cry out to Him in repentance as these men did!

---

[22] Isaiah 6:7

CHAPTER 10

GOD HIMSELF WILL PROVIDE A LAMB

"Behold the Lamb of God who takes away the sin of the world!" exclaimed the forerunner of the Messiah when he saw Jesus.[1] Of all that John might have said of Jesus in an age of heightened Messianic expectancy, he chose this designation before anything else. Just as men tend to view God in their own self-serving image, men are also guilty of picturing the Messiah in the office that most gratifies *them*. So it was in this time of political declension and deep unrest under Gentile rule that most Jews expected the Messiah to come in power and glory, depose the oppressor, establish His own rule and Kingdom, and restore the lost glory of Israel.

There *was* a biblical basis for such expectancy, but it was a partial, incomplete understanding, which omitted the central purpose to His coming, namely, to "save His people from their sins." And this is how Jesus described John:

> …Yes, I say to you, and one who is more than a prophet. This is the one about whom it is written, "Behold, I send My messenger ahead of

---

[1] John 1:29

You, who will prepare Your way before
You."…Among those born of women, there is
no one greater than John [the Baptist]...[2]

It seems utterly significant, then, that John, bypassing
the title of King to describe Jesus, used the least known, the
least understood and the least honored of all the titles with
which he could announce the Messiah. Because of his
proximity to God and separation from the world, he saw by
the Spirit the great significance of Jesus as the Lamb of
God. Our failure to see this, and to appreciate and receive
the benefits that flow from it, will be in exact proportion to
our pride, which repels the Spirit of revelation. Pride has
always concealed from men the centrality of propitiatory
sacrifice. The concept of it is offensive to their
sensibilities. In fact, nothing is more repulsive to modern
men than the idea of such a necessity. It is a *messy*
business to perform, much less to contemplate, and we
would just as soon be disposed to find more suitable
alternatives than to have the displeasure of a Holy God who
intended that we should be discomforted by our sins. It is
fair to say that of all the unique characteristics of the
Judaism of God, this is by far the most odious and
objectionable to the Judaisms of the world.

John the Baptist had no such difficulty; he knew that a
just God needed to be assuaged. It is we who fail to sense
the horror of sin. This again reveals our grievous fault,
namely, we have an absurdly exalted view of our own
righteousness and a pathetically inadequate view of the
Holy and Righteous God. What Job reveals in his painful
acknowledgment of his own state of sinfulness before such
a holy God is incumbent upon us all, "I retract, and I repent
in dust and ashes." The casting of dust and ashes upon
one's head—our crowning glory—is nothing less than the
symbol of burial and death! "The soul who sins will die,"[3]

---

[2] Luke 7:26-28
[3] Ezekiel 18:4

God assures us, and waits for us to agree with His verdict. Blessed is the man who comes to realize it on this side of eternity.

A just God cannot be indifferent to our violation of His laws. Account must be given for the breaking of them, or else they cease to be a viable standard for human conduct— thus opening the way to anarchy and the ultimate disfigurement of His divine image in us. However, let us consider a merciful God:

> Isaac spoke to Abraham his father and said, "My father!" And he said, "Here I am, my son." And he said, "Behold, the fire and the wood, but where is the lamb for the burnt offering?" Abraham said, "God will provide for Himself the lamb for the burnt offering, my son."[4]

There is not a whimper of complaint from either father or son that God's requirement of a burnt offering is in any way unjust. On the contrary, Abraham, instructing his servants to wait before the mount, refers to it as *worship*.[5] Typically, the offering for sin had to be burned by fire; that is, it was a total offering, totally consumed. It had to first be killed by the one for whose sins the lamb was sacrificed in his stead. Would we continue to be so careless about our self-centered and self-righteous ways if we ourselves had to apply the knife to the throat of a hapless lamb?

Abraham's perfect obedience in sacrificing Isaac was not the result of mindless and emotionless senility, but the expression of perfect trust in God. In other words, Abraham consented to the judgments of God. Abraham loved Isaac. What is sacrifice if it should cost us little? This was the child of his old age, the *child of promise*, all that he held most dear, his very life itself! In giving his son, he gave himself; he gave ultimately, and received in like measure as he gave. I cannot help but pause here to

---

[4] Genesis 22:7-8

[5] Ibid., v. 5

suggest to pained Jewish men and women, who, in considering the case for Christ, feel as if they are being asked to sacrifice their *Jewishness*—that which is most familiar and dear. But will not God do for you as He did for Abraham? If you should hear the divine call to a seemingly painful sacrifice and say "Here I am,"[6] as Abraham did, then God will give you much beyond what you sacrifice. It may be that because "you have not withheld,"[7] He will bless you and return to you a fuller Judaism than the one you thought you were being asked to sacrifice!

As indicated before, real faith is not mere mental assent or acknowledgment of God. Real faith is commitment and trust that issues in action. Abraham's faith resulted in trust and obedience:

> Abraham stretched out his hand and took the knife to slay his son. But the angel of the Lord called to him from heaven, and said, "Abraham, Abraham!" And he said, "Here I am." He said, "Do not stretch out your hand against the lad, and do nothing to him; for now I know that you fear God, since you have not withheld your son, your only son, from Me." Then Abraham raised his eyes and looked, and behold, behind him a ram caught in the thicket by his horns; and Abraham went and took the ram and offered him up for a burnt offering in the place of his son.[8]

The substitution of a lamb provided by God is set like the central jewel in the Book of Beginnings. In fact, the account of the man of faith, Abraham, is much like the account of the birth of the nation Israel:

> Now the Lord said to Moses and Aaron in the land of Egypt, "...Speak to all the congregation

---

[6] Ibid., v. 11
[7] Ibid., v. 12
[8] Ibid., vv. 10-13

of Israel, saying, 'On the tenth of this month
they are each one to take a lamb for themselves,
according to their fathers' households, a lamb
for each household. Now if the household is too
small for a lamb, then he and his neighbor
nearest to his house are to take one according to
the number of persons in them; according to
what each man should eat, you are to divide the
lamb. Your lamb shall be an unblemished male
a year old; you may take it from the sheep or
from the goats. You shall keep it until the
fourteenth day of the same month, then the
whole assembly of the congregation of Israel is
to kill it at twilight.'[9]

The purpose of the four-day period between the tenth and
the fourteenth was to keep the lamb available for public
examination, so that any defect that would render it
unusable could be found. The public ministry of Jesus for
almost four years bears a striking similarity to this event, as
does the four-day period between His triumphal entry into
Jerusalem[10] and the time of His crucifixion, which, by the
way, took place at the very hour that the Passover lambs
were being slaughtered in preparation for the Pesach
observance!

Then Moses called for all the elders of Israel and
said to them, "Go and take for yourselves lambs
according to your families, and slay the Passover
lamb. You shall take a bunch of hyssop and dip
it in the blood which is in the basin, and apply
some of the blood that is in the basin to the lintel
and the two doorposts..."[11]

---

[9] Exodus 12:1-6
[10] See Luke 19:28-48
[11] Exodus 12:21-22

What is there in this procedure that has human reason to commend it? Why blood? Why a lamb? Why this particular application? Is this not a bloody and irrational religion? It should not come as a surprise when we know that God chooses the foolish things, the base things, and the despised things to confound the wisdom of man. Pity the Jew who rejected the observation of it that night because it was not part of his tradition, or because he could not see the reason for it. The Lord said, "I will execute judgments—I am the Lord...when I see the blood I will pass over you, and no plague will befall you to destroy you when I strike the land of Egypt."[12] In the ordinance, God commanded Israel to "observe this event forever" and "when your children will say to you, 'What does this rite mean to you?' that you shall say, 'It is a Passover *sacrifice* to the Lord.' "[13]

The primacy of sacrifice with the shedding of blood became, through God's ordinances, the central practice of biblical Judaism from the inception of the wilderness tabernacle to the destruction of the second temple in 70 A.D. The Day of Atonement in that time was far different from that which is currently practiced. "...Atonement shall be made for you to cleanse you; you will be clean from all your sins before the Lord."[14] Atonement means *reconciliation with God*, and was made when the high priest sprinkled the blood of the sacrificed substitute. It was a principle that all understood: *a life for a life*. The offering implied the acknowledgment of sin and the recognition of its just penalty, which was death—so that the death being worked in the one was life for other. The believing Israelite understood that "...it is impossible for the blood of bulls and goats to take away sins."[15] By faith, he anticipated a perfect Atonement to come, to which his

---

[12] Ibid., vv. 12-13
[13] Ibid., see vv. 24-27. Emphasis mine
[14] Leviticus 16:30b
[15] Hebrews 10:4

observances pointed. His faith—that is, his obedience—like Abraham's, was counted to him as righteousness, securing the salvation of God.

In Jewish life today, salvation by faith in the efficacy of the shed blood of a perfect sacrifice, central to the biblical Judaism of God, has fallen into almost complete obsolescence. It is considered an embarrassment in much of modern Christianity and a scandalous, archaic relic in modern Judaism. It is an intolerable offense to human pride and to every system of religion that is based on human merit. When asked about these biblical practices, most rabbis (Gentile as well as Jewish) quickly pass them over as unhappy aspects of a primitive past, while pointing with pride to the more *progressive* developments in Judaism, in keeping with the evolution of *higher* (i.e. more rational) concepts of God. The ultimate logic of such a departure from biblical precepts is the appeal, as I painfully heard at a recent Yom Kippur service, for the purchase of Israel bonds as an appropriate *mitzvah* for the solemn season! However worthy such practices are in themselves, they are completely destitute of the power to save.

> For the life of the flesh is in the blood, and I have given it to you on the altar to make atonement for your souls; for it is the blood by reason of the life that makes atonement.[16]

When has God negated this, or any other word? By what authority do we dare suggest any other alternative? With our Temple destroyed and our priesthood dispersed and lost, what then is the answer to our dilemma? How is it that the God who enjoined us to these sacred practices has also permitted the destruction of the facilities that were necessary for these practices to be observed? Has that perfect Atonement, to which these practices pointed, already been provided? Did God Himself already "provide a lamb"?

---

[16] Leviticus 17:11

CHAPTER 11

THE SUFFERING SERVANT

> Break forth, shout joyfully together, you waste
> places of Jerusalem; for the Lord has comforted
> His people, He has redeemed Jerusalem. The
> Lord has bared *His holy arm* in the sight of all
> the nations, that all the ends of the earth may see
> the salvation of our God.[1]

> Who has believed our message? And to whom
> has *the arm of the Lord* been revealed?[2]

So begins the most profoundly revealing Messianic text in
the entire Old Testament. There are overwhelming
numbers of Jews who have never read these scriptures from
Isaiah. This is an incalculable tragedy for us as a people.
The fact that this sacred portion is omitted from Haftorah
readings in synagogues can scarcely be attributed to
oversight. Rather, have not our rabbis sought to *protect* our
people from being led astray by verses that are suggestive
of Jesus as the Messiah? Surely the meanings of the verses
are self-evident? The phrase *arm of the Lord* indicates an
extension, or a part, of God Himself! There is no doubt

---

[1] Isaiah 52:9-10. Emphasis mine
[2] Isaiah 53:1. Emphasis mine

that this *arm* is a person as well, which is suggested in the following verses:

> ...And for My arm they will wait expectantly...Awake, awake, put on strength, O arm of the Lord; awake as in the days of old, the generations of long ago...Was it not You who dried up the sea, the waters of the great deep; who made the depths of the sea a pathway for the redeemed to cross over...For I am the Lord your God, who stirs up the sea and its waves roar (the Lord of hosts is His name).[3]

"To whom has the arm of the Lord been revealed?" Except God reveal, we cannot see; except we believe His message, He will not reveal!

> For He grew up before Him like a tender shoot, and like a root out of parched ground; He has no stately form or majesty that we should look upon Him, nor appearance that we should be attracted to Him.[4]

Here, the arm of the Lord is revealed as a 'He,' a person. He is an extension of God, even though He is separate and *grew up before* Him. The *parched ground* seems to suggest the spiritually impoverished condition of Israel at the time of His appearing. That He has no form or attractiveness that He should be desired refers not to His natural appearance but to the brutal mistreatment He suffered, as is suggested by this verse:

> ...His appearance was marred more than any man and His form more than the sons of men. Thus [as a result of this and in this condition] He will sprinkle many nations.[5]

---

[3] See Isaiah 51:5-15
[4] Isaiah 53:2
[5] Isaiah 52:14,15

Further suggestions of terrible physical suffering and abuse are found in other parts of the scriptures:

> I gave My back to those who strike Me, and My cheeks to those who pluck out the beard; I did not cover My face from humiliation and spitting.[6]

> He was despised and forsaken of men, a man of sorrows and acquainted with grief; and like one from whom men hide their face He was despised, and we did not esteem Him.[7]

> But I am a worm and not a man, a reproach of men and despised by the people. All who see me sneer at me; they separate with the lip, they wag the head, saying, "Commit yourself to the Lord; let Him deliver him; let Him rescue him, because He delights in him."[8]

> Surely our griefs He Himself bore, and our sorrows He carried; yet we ourselves esteemed Him stricken, smitten of God, and afflicted. But He was pierced through for our transgressions, He was crushed for our iniquities; the chastening for our well-being fell upon Him, and by His scourging we are healed. All of us like sheep have gone astray, each of us has turned to his own way; but the Lord has caused the iniquity of us all to fall on Him.[9]

> And those passing by were hurling abuse at Him, wagging their heads and saying, "You who are going to destroy the temple and rebuild it in three days, save Yourself! If You are the Son of God, come down from the cross." In the same way the chief priests also, along with the scribes

---

[6] Isaiah 50:6
[7] Isaiah 53:3
[8] Psalms 22:6-8
[9] Isaiah 53:4-6

and elders, were mocking Him and saying, "He
saved others; He cannot save Himself. He is the
King of Israel; let Him now come down from the
cross, and we will believe in Him. He trusts in
God; let God rescue Him now, if He delights in
Him; for He said, 'I am the Son of God.' "[10]

Here is the introduction of the meaning of this
unparalleled suffering, namely, the doctrine of vicarious
atonement for all human sin: "The chastening for our well-
being fell upon Him"—also translated, "made the iniquity
of us all to meet on Him." Nor should we fail to observe
that it says, "*the Lord* has caused..." He was "smitten of
God." He received the stroke that was due us, for "He
made Him who knew no sin to be sin on our behalf, so that
we might become the righteousness of God in Him."[11]

Contrary to the ignorant taunts of "Christ-killers,"
uttered for centuries by those who had no real regard for
Him other than grotesque sentimentality, we are clearly
told in the scriptures that His suffering and death was by
the counsel and foreknowledge of God: "[T]his Man,
delivered over by the predetermined plan and
foreknowledge of God, you nailed to a cross by the hands
of godless men and put Him to death."[12] Our fleshly minds
stagger at this; we cannot grasp it, primarily because we
cannot grasp the enormity of our sins that made it
necessary! Even the disciples failed to understand, as these
candid verses reveal:

From that time Jesus began to show His
disciples that *He must go* to Jerusalem, and
suffer many things from the elders and chief
priests and scribes, and be killed, and be raised
up on the third day. Peter took Him aside and
began to rebuke Him, saying, "God forbid it,

---

[10] Matthew 27:39-43
[11] 2 Corinthians 5:21
[12] See Acts 2:22-24

> Lord! This shall never happen to You." But He
> turned and said to Peter, "Get behind Me, Satan!
> You are a stumbling block to Me; for you are
> not setting your mind on God's interests, but
> man's."[13]

For them, as for us, it takes the actual event of His
crucifixion at Golgotha to see in that agony the fulfillment
of God's plan for the ages and the prophetic picture given
in the Psalms and in Isaiah written hundreds of years *before*
the coming of Christ. Before the advent of the Roman Empire, before the possibility of the knowledge of crucifixion
as a form of death, the Spirit of God described in exacting
detail the very suffering and rejection and death for which
the Messiah was destined—and has fulfilled!

> They open wide their mouth at me, as a ravening
> and a roaring lion. I am poured out like water,
> and all my bones are out of joint; my heart is
> like wax; it is melted within me. My strength is
> dried up like a potsherd, and my tongue cleaves
> to my jaws; and *You lay me in the dust of death.*
> For dogs have surrounded me; a band of
> evildoers has encompassed me; they pierced my
> hands and my feet. I can count all my bones.
> They look, they stare at me.[14]

What must have been obscure and mysterious to the
faithful of Israel, who pondered these scriptures through the
centuries, was fulfilled in one stroke and to the last detail in
the coming of the Messiah Jesus, who "must
go…suffer...and be killed." Matthew records that Jesus
quoted the first verse of this psalm while hanging on the
cross: "My God, My God, why hast Thou forsaken Me?"[15]
Even a few unwitting Roman soldiers, who had not so
much as a notion of the meaning of prophecy, fulfilled part

---

[13] Matthew 16:21-23. Emphasis mine
[14] Psalms 22:13-17. Emphasis mine
[15] Matthew 27:46

of that same psalm in so minute a detail as this: "They divide my garments among them, and for my clothing they cast lots."[16] We see this prophecy fulfilled at Golgotha as well:

> And when they had come to a place called Golgotha, which means Place of a Skull, they gave Him wine to drink mingled with gall; and after tasting it, He was unwilling to drink. And when they had crucified Him, they divided up His garments among themselves, casting lots.[17]

This refers to Psalms 69:21, "They also gave me gall for my food and for my thirst they gave me vinegar to drink." In fact, the whole of Psalms 69 contributes to the Messianic tapestry, describing the reproach and humiliation of the servant of God. How ignorant and vain it is to rant about *our* book or *their* book as if the Old and New Testaments are in competition with each other, expressing the separate revelations of rival Gods! Just as there is only one God, there is also only one Book: the Holy Scriptures, from Genesis to Revelation, which alone can make us *wise unto salvation*. It takes the testimony of Christ and the events recorded in the New Testament to provide that framework for which the prophecies and details of the Old are fitted, and without which they make no sense. As someone has aptly said, "The New Testament is in the Old, concealed, and the Old Testament is in the New, revealed." Let us continue on, then, with the Old Testament prophecies, which read as if they had been written beneath the Messiah's cross:

> He was oppressed and He was afflicted, yet He did not open His mouth; like a lamb that is led to slaughter, and like a sheep that is silent before its shearers, so He did not open His mouth.[18]

---

[16] Psalms 22:18
[17] Matthew 27:33-35
[18] Isaiah 53:7; see also Matthew 26:59-63

> By oppression and judgment He was taken away; and as for His generation, who considered that He was cut off out of the land of the living for the transgression of my people, to whom the stroke was due?[19]

Daniel was given a prophetic timetable to indicate when these events were to take place:

> So you are to know and discern that from the issuing of a decree to restore and rebuild Jerusalem until Messiah the Prince there will be seven weeks and sixty-two weeks; it will be built again, with plaza and moat, even in times of distress. Then after the sixty-two weeks the *Messiah will be cut off and have nothing*, and the people of the prince who is to come will destroy the city and the sanctuary.[20]

As the city and sanctuary were destroyed in 70 A.D. by the army of Titus, we ask who then might the Messiah be, who must come before that dreadful event and be 'cut off'? The genealogical records, which alone could prove the Messiah's lineage from David, were also destroyed along with the Temple. With the priesthood dispersed and lost, the altar destroyed, and the sacrifices ceased, by what continuing provision could the Atonement of the people be effected?

> ...All things are cleansed with blood, and without shedding of blood there is no forgiveness...now once at the consummation of the ages He has been manifested to put away sin by the sacrifice of Himself. And inasmuch as it is appointed for men to die once and after this comes judgment, so Christ also, having been offered once to bear the sins of many...[21]

---

[19] Isaiah 53:8
[20] Daniel 9:25-26a. Emphasis mine
[21] Hebrews 9:22-28a

CHAPTER 12

THE RESURRECTED KING

As mentioned, it was not enough simply to kill the Passover lamb; the blood of that non-blemished lamb had to be *applied*: "You shall take a bunch of hyssop and dip it in the blood which is in the basin, and apply some of the blood that is in the basin to the lintel and the two doorposts."[1]

"God will provide for Himself a lamb,"[2] and, like Abraham who "went and took the ram, and offered him up for a burnt offering in the place of his son,"[3] we must actively avail ourselves of God's provision. There is no such thing as passive salvation. Although we can do nothing to earn it, for it is a gift, yet we cannot experience redemption into a land of promise unless we receive it! Something is required of us beyond mere acknowledgment or approval:

> But the Lord was pleased [it was His will] to crush Him, putting Him to grief; if He would render Himself as a guilt offering, He will see

---

[1] Exodus 12:22
[2] Genesis 22:8
[3] Ibid., v. 13

> His offspring, He will prolong His days, and the
> good pleasure of the Lord will prosper in His
> hand. As a result of the anguish of His soul, He
> will see it and be satisfied; by His knowledge the
> Righteous One, My Servant, will justify the
> many, as He will bear their iniquities.
> Therefore, I will allot Him a portion with the
> great, and He will divide the booty with the
> strong; because He poured out Himself to death,
> and was numbered with the transgressors; yet He
> Himself bore the sin of many, and interceded for
> the transgressors.[4]

Truly, "the wages of sin is death, but the free gift of
God is eternal life in Christ Jesus our Lord."[5]   You may
ask, "How is this gift to be received?" If you have come to
see that salvation is of God, that it is to be earnestly desired, and that it can be received only as a gift—for we
have no merit—then that is already to have crossed the
great divide that sets apart the Judaism of God from every
lesser kind. The fact that one cannot earn salvation is a
great blow to the insufferable pride of men.   No
philanthropic deeds or acts of any kind—religious or
charitable—can obtain from God what He has already
wrought.

"For by grace you have been saved through faith; and
that not of yourselves, it is the gift of God; not as a result of
works, so that no one may boast."[6]   This doctrine of
'justification by faith,' which is central to the Judaism of
God, has, no doubt, a *Christian* ring in the ears of untutored
Jews. To us Jews, the word *faith* connotes a kind of easy
believing, a cowardly substitute for real doing! We say,
"Well, anybody can believe or acknowledge certain facts or
principles; it is *doing* that counts!"   With that posture, we

---

[4] Isaiah 53:10-12
[5] Romans 6:23
[6] Ephesians 2:8-9

move from the biblical way of God to the spirit of the world that delights to quote, "God helps them that help themselves," not knowing that it is nowhere to be found in the Bible. Indeed, that philosophy is antithetical to the whole teaching of the Bible.

> For what does the Scripture say? "Abraham believed God, and it was credited to him as righteousness." Now to the one who works, his wage is not credited as a favor, but as what is due. But to the one who does not work, but *believes in Him* who justifies the ungodly, *his faith is credited as righteousness.*[7]
>
> For the promise to Abraham or to his descendants that he would be heir of the world was not through the Law, but through the righteousness of faith. For if those who are of the Law are heirs, faith is made void and the promise is nullified; for the Law brings about wrath, but where there is no law, there also is no violation. For this reason *it is by faith, in order that it may be in accordance with grace*, so that the promise will be guaranteed to all the descendants, not only to those who are of the Law, but also to those who are of the *faith of Abraham*, who is the father of us all.[8]

There is faith, and then, there is true faith; not everyone who professes to believe God actually does. What, then, is the faith of Abraham, the faith that saves? It is the faith that believes in the God who 'gives life to the dead,'[9] the God of resurrection, the supernatural God, the God of power and miracles, the same God who speaks and who fulfills His spoken word.

---

[7] Romans 4:3-5. Emphases mine
[8] Ibid., vv. 13-16. Emphases mine
[9] Ibid., v. 17

In conversation with many of my kinsmen, who profess to believe in God, I learn, to my amazement that most find a way to reject all of His miracles. They have rational explanations for every account of His power. The parting of the Red Sea is seen as a "shifting of the tides." The conception of Jesus by the Virgin Mary is considered to be the work of a "Roman Solider." But the faith of the Judaism of God is the faith that believes God according to His Word—that He who spoke it will also perform it. This kind of faith often brings condescending looks from both *religious* people and others, who, in their wise conceits, have demythologized the scriptures. They are adamant in their assurance that it is no great matter anyway, because God is certainly not interested in such insignificant things, and only wants us to be good and do what is right.

However much these attitudes may be sufficient for the Judaisms of men, they constitute the effectual rejection of the God of Abraham, the God of Israel, the only true and Living God. If we only had eyes to see the varieties of practical atheism that infest the religious world! To see that the rejection of God's Word is really the rejection of God Himself! To see that the *unwillingness* to have Him as Lord, to obey Him and to follow Him, is at the root of all our unbelief!

We can only begin to fathom the superb wisdom of God who requires that there be only two things that constitute our salvation—if we receive them by faith: that Jesus is Lord, and that God has raised Him from the dead. Paul says that "if you confess with your mouth Jesus as Lord, and believe in your heart that God raised Him from the dead, you will be saved."[10]

Note the emphasis here on our voluntary will to "confess...and believe." It is as though God expects the scriptures to be more than sufficient to establish these matters of the faith, and all that is required is both the will to live by them, and also the consent to the great price that

---

[10] Romans 10:9

one pays for such obedience. Obedience to the Father cost Jesus rejection, suffering and death; and the fate of His disciples is well known. The Judaisms of the world are far more convenient, full of plaudits, honors and flattery for men, but they do not save. It is a matter of choice, and when *you* choose which Judaism *you* will subscribe to, choose carefully because, "whatever a man sows, this he will also reap."[11]

Surely, resurrection is the belief most taxing to our modern mindset. To bring one back from the dead is the supreme manifestation of supernatural power. As the scriptures so candidly depict, even the disciples staggered in unbelief, failing to remember the repeated assurances of their Master that He would be resurrected on the third day, according to the scriptures. Interestingly, the *adversaries* of Jesus remembered this remarkable claim, and hasted to Pilate to have the tomb secured:

> …Sir, we remember that when He was still alive that deceiver said, "After three days I am to rise again." Therefore, give orders for the grave to be made secure until the third day, otherwise the disciples may come and steal Him away and say to the people, "He has risen from the dead," and the last deception will be worse than the first."[12]

Note, for the sake of your own salvation, the extremity of choices that are available to you: the fact that His adversaries referred to, "while He was still alive." This shows that they had no doubt that He was really dead. You must either agree with their suspicions regarding Jesus and the apostles, or believe the resurrection account that follows! They quote Jesus saying, "I will rise again"! What Jesus *said* is always the issue. The same men complained to Pilate for having posted a sign above the cross in Hebrew, Greek and Latin: *Jesus of Nazareth, the*

---

[11] Galatians 6:7
[12] Matthew 27:63-64

King of the Jews: "So the chief priests of the Jews were saying to Pilate, 'Do not write, "The King of the Jews"; but that He said, "I am King of the Jews." '[13]

In Luke's account of the resurrection, the women who came on the third day to prepare His body, believing He was dead, found an empty tomb attended by two celestial messengers who said to them,

> "Why do you seek the living One among the dead?   He is not here, but He has risen. Remember how He spoke to you while He was still in Galilee, saying that the Son of Man must be delivered into the hands of sinful men, and be crucified, and the third day rise again."[14]

The chief priests and elders' response to the news of the empty tomb is very significant.   Again, no middle ground is afforded to us in our extremity of choices.   In Matthew, we learn that when the stunned soldiers who had guarded the tomb reported the supernatural events to the chief priests and elders:

> [T]hey gave a large sum of money to the soldiers, and said, 'You are to say, "His disciples came by night and stole Him away while we were asleep." '[15]

We see the absurdity of this crude fabrication when we read about Jesus' terrified disciples, all of whom deserted their Master and locked themselves in a room—fearful, lest they suffer His fate.   Not only is it unlikely that such cowardly men would attempt to steal Jesus' body right in front of the Roman guards, but it is also irrational to think they would succeed in getting past these guards who had been put there especially for the purpose of watching out for them.   Great is the torment in eternity for those who chose to concoct this tale rather than repent before God at

---

[13] John 19:21
[14] Luke 24:5b-7
[15] Matthew 28:12b,13

the news that what 'that deceiver' said had come true. We are responsible for what we choose to believe, and, unhappily, most people choose to believe this tale. We read on: "And they took the money and did as they had been instructed; and this story was widely spread among the Jews, and is to this day."[16]

How perfectly Jesus has fulfilled what was prophesied over him by the aged Simeon when he was brought as an infant to the temple:

> And Simeon blessed them and said to Mary His mother, "Behold, this Child is appointed for the fall and rise of many in Israel, and for a sign to be opposed—and a sword will pierce even your own soul—to the end *that thoughts from many hearts may be revealed."*[17]

We can draw the conclusion from these words that our response to His resurrection is the ultimate revelation of the deepest secrets of our hearts. When the women who found the empty tomb relayed the astounding information to the disciples, it is recorded that, "…these words appeared to them as nonsense, and *they would not believe them.*"[18]

And then we read that after Christ appeared to Mary Magdalene,

> She went and reported to those who had been with Him, while they were mourning and weeping. When they heard that He was alive and had been seen by her, *they refused to believe it.* After that, He appeared in a different form to two of them while they were walking along on their way to the country. They went away and reported it to the others, but *they did not believe them either.*[19]

---

[16] Ibid., v. 15
[17] Luke 2:34,35. Emphasis mine
[18] Luke 24:11b. Emphasis mine
[19] Mark 16:10-13. Emphases mine

The candor of these admissions speaks profoundly for the truth of the resurrection of Jesus Christ. If these things were not true, certainly any group of men attempting to pass off so colossal a fraud upon the world would not so mindlessly have revealed their own cowardice, betrayal, fear and unbelief. Even when they were confronted by the resurrected Christ, we read,

> When they saw Him, they worshiped Him; *but some were doubtful.*[20]

> While they were telling these things, He Himself stood in their midst and said to them, "Peace be to you." But *they were startled and frightened* and thought that they were seeing a spirit.[21]

> But Thomas, one of the twelve, called Didymus, was not with them when Jesus came. So the other disciples were saying to him, "We have seen the Lord!" But he said to them, "Unless I shall see in His hands the imprint of the nails, and put my finger into the place of the nails, and put my hand into His side, I will not believe."[22]

Here we see a sample of the catalog of doubt, fear and even stubborn, willful unbelief, which the resurrected Christ revealed in men. Our will, the center of our autonomy and our very being, is crucial to the matter of faith, as we will examine in the next chapter. Jesus Himself suggests this in His response to the unbelieving Thomas:

> After eight days His disciples were again inside, and Thomas with them. Jesus came, the doors having been shut, and stood in their midst and said, "Peace be with you." Then He said to Thomas, "Reach here with your finger, and see My hands; and reach here your hand and put it

---

[20] Matthew 28:17. Emphasis mine
[21] Luke 24:36,37. Emphasis mine
[22] John 20:24,25

into My side; and do not be unbelieving, but believing." Thomas answered and said to Him, "My Lord and my God!"[23]

---

[23] John 20:26-28

CHAPTER 13

THE DISCIPLES COMMISSION

"Oh, Art, I really admire your faith," I was told one day by an unbelieving colleague to whom I had expressed my new-found convictions. He had known me as a vehement atheist, and now heartily approved my 'good fortune,' much as one would admiringly applaud a person who had a talent for music or art. "I wish I could have a faith like that!" he exclaimed wistfully, but not too sadly, mindful of the weight of responsibility that would attend faith. Despite all my protestations that it was as available to him as it was to me, he airily waved me aside assured that it was just 'one of those passing things.'

How unjust God would be if salvation by faith were just a caprice, available for some and not for others. "Be not unbelieving, but believing," Jesus exhorted Thomas, implying that it is a matter of choice and will. All of His utterances to His disciples concerning His resurrection are rich in instruction for us, as when Jesus drew alongside two crestfallen disciples returning to their home in Emmaus on the resurrection morning, completely oblivious to the fact that the man who walked with them was their resurrected Lord!

And He said to them, "What are these words that you are exchanging with one another as you are walking?" And they stood still, looking sad. One of them, named Cleopas, answered and said to Him, "Are You the only one visiting Jerusalem and unaware of the things which have happened here in these days?" And He said to them, "What things?" And they said to Him, "The things about Jesus the Nazarene, who was a prophet mighty in deed and word in the sight of God and all the people, and how the chief priests and our rulers delivered Him to the sentence of death, and crucified Him. But we were hoping that it was He who was going to redeem Israel. Indeed, besides all this, it is the third day since these things happened. But also some women among us amazed us. When they were at the tomb early in the morning, and did not find His body, they came, saying that they had also seen a vision of angels who said that He was alive. Some of those who were with us went to the tomb and found it just exactly as the women also had said; but Him they did not see."[1]

The statement is so remarkably revealing that I quote the whole of it. Note the terrible dejection and disappointment it expresses in their fond Messianic hopes for the restoration of the glory of Israel, and in their stead, a battered, dead Master, "...marred more than any man and His form more than the sons of men."[2] Not even the report of an empty tomb, on the third day, could stir a ray of hope. Even the report of the angels seems incredulous to them. All they now had was to look forward to a life of restored normality after the public cooled down, and perhaps have

---

[1] Luke 24:17-24
[2] Isaiah 52:14b

fond reminiscences with each other in the years ahead when they should chance to meet.

They are one in kind with the women who lovingly came to the tomb so early in the morning with their spices and tears to embalm His body. Their secret hearts were not so anxious to meet a live Christ, who challenges us to: "Go into all the world and preach the gospel to all creation."[3]

The world much prefers embalming Jesus to obeying Him. It prefers the sweet spices of sentimentality and pity; it would rather see Jesus in His passion, stretched out on their crucifixes, rather than risen, alive and challenging. It prefers solemn masses, moving intonations, processions, mourning, black crepe, incense, beads, ritual—in a word, *religion*. The world prefers a dead Christ, which implies a harmless Christ; it prefers a name to intone propitiously in order to sanctify marriages and burials of those who never had any other intention but to live as gods unto themselves. "Why do you seek the living One among the dead? He is not here, but He has risen."[4] There is little wonder that Jesus, who knows our hearts, answered His disciples as He did:

> O foolish men and slow of heart to believe in all that the prophets have spoken! Was it not necessary for the Christ to suffer these things and to enter into His glory?" Then beginning with Moses and with all the prophets, He explained to them the things concerning Himself in all the Scriptures.[5]

Peter, when he heard that his Master must suffer and die, retorted, "God forbid it, Lord! This shall never happen to You." Jesus response to him was, "...You are not

---

[3] Mark 16:15
[4] Luke 24:5b-6a
[5] Ibid., vv. 25-27

setting your mind on God's interests but man's."[6] What Peter was really saying, and he speaks for us all, was, "This shall never happen to *me*!" How we shrink from self-denial, suffering, sacrifice and death. Our every impulse is to seek glory for ourselves, but suffering is inescapable when we walk the way of God.

Jesus added, "If anyone wishes to come after Me, let him deny himself, and take up his cross, and follow Me."[7] As there was a necessary crown of thorns before the crown of glory for the Messiah, so it will be for all who will follow Him. Jesus called His disciples "slow of heart," indicating again that belief is a moral matter. Their failure to see the necessity for the crown of thorns was the result of their unwillingness to wear it. We have just as much truth and light as we are willing to bear the suffering necessary to obtain it. Have we been unable to find the truth, or have we unconsciously shrunk from what the truth will mean for us?

---

[6] See Matthew 16:22,23
[7] Matthew 16:24

ADDENDUM

THE CHOSEN PEOPLE – CHOSEN FOR WHAT?

EXAMINING THE JEWISH PREDICAMENT IN AN INCREASINGLY HOSTILE WORLD

As Jews, one thing that makes us recoil is being called "chosen." It is something like the involuntary shudder that comes with the screech of chalk on a blackboard. After all, what has being chosen ever meant to us but trouble? Better that the term had never been coined for all the good it has done us! Where does it come from anyway? Can't we be left alone to live like other people without the ominous overtones that have always dogged us? Chosen for what? Why give to those who instinctively don't like us yet further provocation and pretext for bitterness?

Perhaps you yourself, dear reader, are so reflecting even now. The litany of daily disasters with reports of suicide bombings and the increase of anti-Semitic episodes virtually everywhere in the world give us a heightened sense of dread. What will the end of all this be? Is this what it means to be a Jew? How long before we will fear for our children, or ourselves, on the streets of America's cities and suburbs?

Is the answer to be more assertive and more insistent on our rights as citizens—demanding that public officials guarantee our safety? Or, is it to be found in supporting Jewish organizations who have access to policy makers in government or influence in the media, and who monitor the activity of hate groups?

In former times of distress, our more religious kinsmen would sigh, "When Messiah comes..." How plaintive, if not pathetic, to make that an appeal now! That frail expectation saved no one in the Nazi Holocaust of World War II. Can even the *Chasidim*, who daily gather up into plastic bags the grisly, severed members of nail-torn bomb victims, sustain such a hope? What real defense do we have when America's proudest commercial towers are not exempt from attack? This vitriolic hatred, infecting even children, at first against "Zionists," and now Jews in every place, threatens us all.

If There is a God, Where is He Now?

From the vantage point of our historic and present Jewish life, the evidence of a living God does seem painfully sparse. If there is such a God, how are we to interpret or understand His apparent, palpable absence? Perhaps from a biblical perspective, one might even suggest that He has a controversy with us, or has withdrawn His Presence, in proportion to our own indifference and alienation from Him. This is a supposition which the scriptures, of which we have characteristically little knowledge or interest, seem to suggest.

The very first chapter of the Book of Proverbs sends the chilling message that because we refused the call of wisdom, she will even laugh at our calamity and mock when dread comes upon us like a storm; and it will be too late because: "they hated knowledge and did not choose the fear of the Lord...But he who listens to me [wisdom] shall live securely and will be at ease from the dread of evil."[1]

By and large, are we not Torah indifferent, preferring to bury ourselves in literature of entirely other kinds, as in the copious folds of a Sunday Times and the like—all of which uniformly espouse views antagonistic to faith? The very idea of divine authorship, that is, Scripture actually inspired by God, is contrary and offensive to our incredulous, secular minds. We instantly, matter-of-factly and self-evidently dismiss it out of hand—no discussion necessary.

Though the Hebrew prophets proclaimed, "Thus says the Lord," and Isaiah announced, in commencing his book, a vision which he saw concerning Judah and Jerusalem, we are persuaded, together with our more liberal rabbis, that such are altogether stylistic devices and quaint rhetoric peculiar to the Bible as literature.

A remarkably candid statement about this unbelief to which we have come as a people is found in a recent article[2] by conservative rabbi and scholar, Alan J. Yuter. *Etz Hayim* is the recently published Torah commentary by a panel of the best scholars and rabbis of Conservative Judaism. Yuter describes *Etz Hayim* as:

> The most ambitious non-Orthodox Jewish Bible Commentary ever written for synagogue use in the history of Jewry, but framed in a modern world view that appropriates ancient ideas that are comfortably usable in modernity.[3]

In commending this new work, Yuter informs us,

> As modernists who reject pre-modern dogma, Conservative Judaism assumes that the Torah's

---

[1] See Porverbs 1: 20-33
[2] *Etz Hayim?—Torah For Our Times: Conservative Judaism's Spiritual Response to Judaism's Canon* (Midstream, May/June 2002).
[3] Ibid., page 21

human language can, by definition, be *no more than the work of human beings...*creating stories that make religious statements. *For Etz Hayim, the Torah is not history but pious, inspirational fiction...God as the hero of Scripture and as a mental and literary construct...God is no more than the power within us that makes for good, salvation, and redemption. There is thus a theological disconnect between the God of Hebrew Scripture,* who "appears" as a real being in the Scriptural text, and *the God idea* of *Etz Hayim's* elite community.[4]

He goes on to say,

For...Conservative Judaism, *holiness and sanctification are a mental mood and not the consequence of obeying the Divine command...*Etz Hayim exhibits intellectual integrity, *but without the religious faith that the classical tradition mandates...The Torah informs but does not command the autonomous moral conscience of the modern liberal Jew...Its religion is not the religion of the Talmud or Bible, but a modern world view that appropriates ancient ideas that are comfortably usable in modernity.*[5]

Evidently, autonomous man, in his mood and disposition, considers himself to be the measure of all things. This asserts the God of Israel to be a figment of Man's imagination! It portrays the giants of our heritage as mere victims of delusion. What is staggering here is the "up-front" boldness, nay even a *boasting,* of these views. This is a proud assertion of the primacy of man over God; of the superiority of an elite council of scholars whose *intuited inspiration* determines for us what is "comfortably

---

[4] Ibid., page 19. Emphases mine
[5] Ibid., page 20, 21. Emphases mine

usable" in modernity! As any superficial assessment of
Scripture will indicate—from the call of Abraham, to the
epochal suffering of Moses, to the Prophets and the
Psalmists—not comfort, but *obedience,* has been the
enduring motif of biblical faith!

By making Man supreme, have we not laid ourselves
open to assault on every side for the forfeiture of just that
faith, inviting the very penalties of covenantal disobedience
for which we were *forewarned* through Moses and the
Prophets? How can we demand the protection of society
from the anti-Semitic attacks that our own unbelief may
have occasioned? Are we so thoroughly secularized as to
be unable to see in our increasing calamities a *divine* cause?
Can we not consider the fact that anti-Semitism pre-dates
Christianity, and has haunted us in every place and time
and nation as being, perhaps, the consequence of
covenantal defection? Or even, the very *evidence* of that
defection?

As Jews, the Chosen of God, the recipients of the
tablets of the Law on Mt. Sinai, the descendants of the
Patriarchs and heirs of the Prophets, should we not
reasonably look *first* for an explanation for our distresses in
a failed relationship with the God of our Fathers, *before*
considering secular, social or political causes?

Are we aware of Moses' warnings in the book of
Deuteronomy[6] in regard to covenantal failure? If we will
not heed God's Word, must we not learn and be instructed
through our bitter experience? As abiding as our distresses
are, they are no less abiding than the reality of God and the
application of His Word! What is this "modernity" to
which all things must be submitted? Is it not the very
'golden calf of idolatry' that has been our undoing from the
very inception of our history as a people? Not only do we
bow to it, we could realistically be called the corrupters of

---

[6] See Deuteronomy 31:29; 32:18 and following.

others, even as we ourselves are corrupted. Is this not perversely contradicting our call to be a "kingdom of priests"[7] and a "light to the nations"[8]?

The Jewish Predicament

Every analysis and critique of "the Jewish predicament" will fall short if it does not factor in this inescapable call to the nations. From the beginning, our purpose was to be a *witness* of the One, True, Living God and Creator King to *all* the nations, and *in* all the nations. Ought we not to suffer proportionate retribution from that God for our willful failure to demonstrate that witness?

If the biblical principle, "As the priests, so also the people" is valid, can't we then say, *as Israel goes, so go the nations?* Is it for our failure as a priestly nation that some measure of resentment, even unconsciously, is kindled against us among the nations? Only a biblically-formed mind could conceivably think this way! Contrary and offensive though it might be to our norms of thought, could such a view be closer to God's? Could we be held liable for our failure to align our thoughts with His? We read in Isaiah,

> "For My thoughts are not your thoughts, nor are your ways My ways," declares the Lord. "For as the heavens are higher than the earth, so are My ways higher than your ways and My thoughts than your thoughts."[9]

If denying His truth distorts reality, perverts life and damages all the processes of living, what *judgment* could issue from a God, who is being so misrepresented, upon

---

[7] Exodus 19:6
[8] Isaiah 42:6
[9] Isaiah 55:8-9

that nation privileged to make Him known? Certainly, God's continuing controversy with us, the Jewish people, is an index of His larger contention with all mankind; but the wider conflict likely awaits resolution first between God and "Israel, His son, His firstborn."[10]

Can it be that our effectual atheism, reflected in a liberally-oriented Judaism, springs from the absence of an actual experience of God *by the Spirit?* Or that our inability to experience God is, in itself, a *judgment of God?* A condition held for so long that it is now considered normative?

Those who reduce God to a "concept" have no God *personally* whom they can seek. One experience of God, as God, dissolves all our doubts! How shall we ever be able to understand, as did the Patriarchs and Prophets of our own faith, that we stand or fall in direct proportion to a true, experiential knowledge of God *as God?*

In its absence, we will find ourselves reducing God to no more than primitive anthropomorphisms, syncretism, and the influence of "other Near Eastern mythologies!" Miracles are 'explained,' and predictive prophecy, robbed of its revelatory power, is dismissed through ingenious alterations in time-line dating! If we are offended by the supernatural, how then can God be God?

Hadn't we better confront these issues on this side of eternity rather than on the other? Will we learn too late our God-rejecting error, when it will be unalterably fixed— eternally and without remedy? How shall we not be unspeakably ashamed for the triviality of a lifestyle that pores over stocks and bonds, or their equivalent, but omits the question of God Himself? For, as the scriptures say,

---

[10] Exodus 4:22

The wicked, in the haughtiness [pride] of his
countenance, does not seek *Him*. All his
thoughts are, "There is no God."[11]

The Undoing of Pride

Such a disposition renders God a negligible object, making
the knowledge of Him irrelevant. The problem is *pride*, the
unduly exalted opinion of one's self! A scholar of an
earlier generation superbly comments on the above verses,

> [Pride] is therefore impatient of a rival, hates a
> superior, and cannot endure a master. In
> proportion as it prevails in the heart, it makes us
> wish to see nothing above us, to acknowledge no
> law but our own wills, to follow no rule but our
> own inclinations. Thus it led Satan to rebel
> against his Creator, and our first parents to
> desire to be as gods. Since such are the effects
> of pride, such a Being as God, One who is
> infinitely powerful, just and holy, who can
> neither be resisted, deceived or deluded, who
> disposes according to His own sovereign
> pleasure, of all creatures and events, and who, in
> an especial manner, hates pride,...is determined
> to abase and punish it...
>
> [Toward] such a Being, pride can contemplate
> only with a feeling of dread, aversion and
> abhorrence. It must look upon Him as its natural
> enemy...These truths torture the proud,
> unhumbled hearts of the wicked, and hence they
> hate that knowledge of God which teaches these
> truths, and will not seek it. On the contrary, they
> wish to remain ignorant of such a Being, and to

---

[11] Psalms 10:4. Emphases mine

banish all thoughts of Him from their minds. With this view they neglect, pervert, or explain away those passages of revelation which describes God's true character, and endeavor to believe that He is altogether such a one as themselves.[12]

This commentator continues,

He [the unhumbled] never takes God or His will into consideration or consultation, to square and frame all accordingly, but proceeds and goes on in all as if there were no God to be consulted...no more than if He were no God; the thought of Him and His will sway him not. Such a God is not of their counsel, is not in the plot; nor is God in their purposes or advising; they do all without Him...all their thought is, that there is no God...[and] seeing there is no God or power above them to take notice of it, to regard or requite them, therefore they may be bold to go on.[13]

We have taken the liberty of inserting these lengthy quotes because they are so rare. Our own age is steeped in unbelief, so normative and unquestioned, as to taint the very air we breathe. To "seek after God" has rarely been commended to us. Indeed, who could do so? It would imply that there is a God who could be found, and who, being a Person, desires to be sought! Such a conviction would be enough to dismiss such an individual from polite society as clearly out of touch with 'reality.'

Yet, is this not the very neglect of God that Israel's own prophets have always protested to an unwilling nation? The covenant given at Mount Sinai, from which we have

---

[12] From Charles H. Spurgeon's *The Treasury of David - A Commentary on the Psalms,* Hendrickson Publishers, Vol.1, pp 117-118.

[13] Ibid., p118.

shrunk, is no icy piece of contractual formalism, but a covenant framed in love by the God who brought us out of Egypt, desiring to have us for His own:

> Moses went up to God, and the LORD called to him from the mountain, saying, "Thus you shall say to the house of Jacob and tell the sons of Israel: 'You yourselves have seen what I did to the Egyptians, and how I bore you on eagles' wings, and brought you to Myself. Now then, if you will indeed obey My voice and keep My covenant, then you shall be My own possession among all the peoples [nations], for all the earth is Mine; and you shall be to Me a kingdom of priests and a holy nation.' "[14]

Pause for a moment and ponder this promise. By its very nature, it requires a vital knowledge and love of God to keep it, which is why He needs to be continually sought! Psalms 25:14 makes it clear that the fear of the Lord is the condition for having the covenant revealed to us. How great our need for the "new" or everlasting covenant spoken of in Jeremiah 31:31-33 and Ezekiel 36:26—a covenant promising "a new heart" and "a new spirit"; a covenant under which God declares that He will write His law on our hearts!

As our distresses mount, how much more should we seriously ponder the word of God in the Psalms, where we are told that:

> The Lord also will be a stronghold for the oppressed, a stronghold in times of trouble; and those who know Your name will put their trust in You, for You, O LORD, have not forsaken those who seek You.[15]

---

[14] Exodus 19:3-6
[15] Psalms 9:9-10

To *know His name* is to experience God in His essential attributes, an intimacy only available to those who seek Him! Can it be that the frustrating helplessness of a besieged Israel is the urgent wake-up call of God to an essentially God-rejecting nation?—who, according to His promise, will not forsake those who put their trust in Him.

However horrific the means, can our increasing predicament be understood as a mercy to save us from yet worse catastrophe?

Lest we assume that personal, ethical morality can substitute for a relationship with God, this writer terrifyingly makes clear:

> The moral who are not devout, the honest who are not prayerful, the benevolent who are not believing, the amiable who are not converted, these must all have their portion with the openly wicked in the hell which is prepared for the devil and his angels...The forgetters of God are far more numerous than the profane or profligate, and according to the very forceful expression in the Hebrew, the nethermost hell will be the place into which all of them shall be hurled headlong.[16]

"The wicked will return to Sheol [Hell], *even* all the nations who forget God," declares Psalms 9:17. As Spurgeon concludes, "Forgetfulness seems a small sin, but it brings eternal wrath upon the man who lives and dies in it."[17] Such a *willful forgetfulness* is, as the psalmist says, *wicked.* "...[F]or where the God of heaven is not, the lord of hell is reigning and raging; and if God not be in our thoughts, our thoughts will bring us to perdition."[18]

---

[16] From Charles H. Spurgeon's *The Treasury of David – A Commentary on the Psalms,* Hendrickson Publishers, Vol.1, pp.100-101
[17] Ibid., p.101
[18] Ibid., p.112

The same "wicked," according to verse 3 of Psalms 10, bless "the greedy man." And greed or covetousness, this root of idolatry, which the tenth commandment condemns, serves to dull the conscience against God. At its heart lies the desire for riches and material acquisition, the desire to unduly possess and to obtain. Every reasonable observer of contemporary Jewish life will acknowledge that this is more descriptive of us than the desire for God—and, indeed, truth to tell, has even become *our* distinctive!

The Rejection of God

If Scripture authenticates itself in the heart of every reader who loves and respects truth, must not our history as Jews reveal the tragic story of so cataclysmic a forfeiture as the rejection of God?

How far will this yet continuing rejection pursue us as misfortune—as the baleful reports of grisly tragedies in Israel and rising anti-Semitism among the nations suggest? Losing our covenant consciousness as a people has not relieved us of its responsibilities—or its stated penalties. Moses included us, as with all previous generations of Jews, at Mt. Sinai:

> Now not with you alone am I making this covenant and this oath [i.e., its *blessings* in obedience and its *curses* in failure], but both with those who stand here with us today in the presence of the LORD our God *and with those who are not with us here today...*[19]

According to Scripture, God anticipates a future recognition from us that will come when we will rightly view our calamities in this covenantal context:

---

[19] Deuteronomy 29:14-15. Emphasis mine

> So it shall be when all of these things have come
> upon you, the blessing and the curse which I
> have set before you, and you call *them* to mind
> in all nations where the LORD your God has
> banished you, and you return to the Lord your
> God and obey Him with all your heart and soul
> according to all that I command you today, you
> and your sons, then the LORD your God will
> restore you from captivity, and have compassion
> on you, and…will circumcise your heart and the
> heart of your descendants, to love the LORD
> your God with all your heart and with all your
> soul, so that you may live.[20]

It is apparent, considering our present condition, that
this "circumcision" of our hearts is yet future. What is not
apparent to us, and far removed from our secular
consciousness, is the recognition of this word as *actually
being God's word.* It shows that our disasters issue from a
rejection of God, remedied only by our return to Him in
genuine repentance! To this, virtually all the prophets
testify:

> For I will be like a lion to Ephraim and like a
> young lion to the house of Judah. I, even I, will
> tear to pieces and go away, I will carry away,
> and there will be none to deliver. I will go away
> and return to My place, *until they acknowledge
> their guilt* and seek My face; in their *affliction*
> they will earnestly seek Me.[21]

---

[20] Deuteronomy 30:1-3a, 6
[21] Hosea 5:14-15. Emphases mine

God's Answer to the Jewish Predicament

In the light of our predicament, are we now willing to look at that single most riveting Messianic prophecy, which gives every appearance of being rabbinically excluded, for obvious reasons, from synagogue Haftorah readings: Isaiah 52:13 through to 53:1-12? Should not read it as if our *life* depended upon it?

> Behold, My servant will prosper, He will be high and lifted up and greatly exalted. Just as many were astonished at you, My people, so His appearance was marred more than any man and His form more than the sons of men. Thus He will sprinkle many nations, kings will shut their mouths on account of Him; for what had not been told them they will see, and what they had not heard they will understand.

> Who has believed our message? And to whom has the arm of the Lord been revealed? For He grew up before Him like a tender shoot, and like a root out of parched ground; He has no stately form or majesty that we should look upon Him, nor appearance that we should be attracted to Him. He was despised and forsaken of men, a man of sorrows and acquainted with grief; and like one from whom men hide their face He was despised, and we did not esteem Him.

> Surely our griefs He himself bore, and our sorrows He carried; yet we ourselves esteemed Him stricken, smitten of God, and afflicted. But He was pierced through for our transgressions, He was crushed for our iniquities; the chastening for our well-being fell upon Him, and by His scourging we are healed. All of us like sheep have gone astray, each of us has turned to His

own way; but the LORD has caused the iniquity of us all to fall on Him.

He was oppressed and He was afflicted, yet He did not open His mouth; like a lamb that is led to slaughter, and like a sheep that is silent before its shearers, so He did not open His mouth. By oppression and judgment He was taken away; and as for His generation, who considered that He was cut off out of the land of the living for the transgression of my people, to whom the stroke was due? His grave was assigned with wicked men, yet He was with a rich man in His death, because He had done no violence, nor was there any deceit in His mouth.

But the Lord was pleased to crush Him, putting Him to grief; if He would render Himself as a guilt offering, He will see His offspring, He will prolong His days, and the good pleasure of the Lord will prosper in His hand. As a result of the anguish of His soul, He will see it and be satisfied; by His knowledge the Righteous One, My Servant, will justify the many, as He will bear their iniquities. Therefore, I will allot Him a portion with the great, and He will divide the booty with the strong; because He poured out Himself to death, and was numbered with the transgressors; yet He Himself bore the sin of many, and interceded for the transgressors.[22]

Of whom does this speak? Many Jewish authorities have insisted that it describes the redemptive suffering of the Jewish nation itself. Certainly it is suggestive of much of our historical experience, and perhaps more ominously, that which is yet to come. But who is the "He" who is despised and forsaken of men, and the "we" who have hid

---

[22] Isaiah 52:13 - 53:12

our faces from Him? Who is the "He" who bore "our" griefs, who was pierced through for "our" transgressions, crushed for "our" iniquities? Are we not the sheep who have gone astray, turning every one to our own way? Has not the Lord caused the iniquity of us all to fall on *Him?*

Do consider that this prophecy was written seven centuries before the advent of the Galilean, Jesus of Nazareth, and even before the formation of the Roman Empire, whose distinctive execution through crucifixion this Sufferer is evidently bearing.[23] Surely, in Isaiah 53, it could not be said of us Jews that we "...had done no violence, nor was there any deceit in His [our] mouth," since it was because of *the transgression of My people* to whom the stroke was due.[24]

He will *be satisfied* evidently signals this servant's life-after-death continuation! Indeed, everything hinges upon the *resurrection* of this Suffering Servant. However unfamiliar this is to us, it is nevertheless not *Christian*, or Gentile *per se,* but indisputably biblical!

Could our difficulty with the *goyish* New Testament be our failure to perceive what had preceded it, what had actually been foretold in our own Hebrew scriptures? Having failed in the first, a failure *that yet prevails,* must we not necessarily fail in the other? The unbroken continuum of the two Testaments is lost to us *because we have not adequately embraced the first!*

Are we not still refusing, now as then, to consider the exhortation of the despised Galilean to His rejecting contemporaries to search the Jewish scriptures, of which He Himself said, "it is these that testify about Me"[25]? He declared that if we had *believed Moses, we would believe*

---

[23] Consider the graphic details of death by crucifixion, astonishingly recorded a thousand years before the event, and described in Psalms 22

[24] Isaiah 53:8

[25] John 5:39

Him, for Moses wrote of Him.[26]   Could it be that our mounting troubles are again a consequence of that very same stubborn inconsideration?

Grace and Law

Consider the unfamiliar opening statement of the Gospel of John: "For the Law was given through Moses; grace and truth were realized through Jesus [the] Christ [*Christ* in Greek, *Y'Shua Ha Mashiach* in Hebrew]."[27]

Could it be that the Law's demands, requiring our complete observance, are intended to bring us before God in an acknowledged, broken dependency? This recognition would necessarily then precede the enablement given by the same God as a "gift" (grace) to those who seriously seek *righteousness* with God through the Law, but necessarily fail to obtain it. Therefore the New Testament says,

> He came to His own, and those who were His own did not receive Him. But as many as received Him, to them He gave the right [authority] to become children [sons] of God, even to those who believe in His name.[28]

In his Letter to the Romans, Paul, the Jewish apostle, brilliantly explicates the connection between the Law given through Moses and the grace that came through Jesus,

> ...so that the requirement of the Law [Torah] might be fulfilled in us, who do not walk according to the flesh [a rules-guided, human determination to fulfill divine commandments],

---

[26] See John 5:46
[27] John 1:17
[28] John 1:11-12

> *but according to the Spirit...*and those who are
> in the flesh cannot please God.[29]

For Paul, as for Jesus, the Law is holy and is not to be abrogated or annulled. Rather, Jesus says, "Do not think that I came to abolish the Law or the Prophets; I did not come to abolish but to fulfill."[30]

Unhappily, much of historic Christianity has lost, rejected, or never understood its continuity with its Hebrew roots. Tragically, this has served to discourage us, as Jews, from even considering the place of Jesus in our Jewish heritage.

What we would suggest now, though it flies in the face of our deepest Jewish prejudices, is that though the Church that historically bears His name has shamefully misrepresented Him, the issue of this "messianic pretender" is, more than we are presently able to realize, the very issue of God. Life and death are decided by one's own disposition toward Him! Never has so much hung, then, on the recognition of a single person!

The recognition of these truths, as well as their fulfillment to us, waits upon a bestowal of God's Spirit, *Ruach,* promised to us by the Prophets—the very medium of Divine revelation and empowerment for which our scholarly and rabbinical elites are an inadequate substitute! Jesus mystified a sincerely inquiring Nicodemus, "a ruler of the Jews," when He said,

> Truly, truly, I say to you, unless one is born of
> water [the Word of God] and the Spirit he
> cannot enter into the kingdom of God. That
> which is born of the flesh is flesh, but that which
> is born of the Spirit is spirit...Are you the

---

[29] Romans 8:4, 8. Emphasis mine
[30] Matthew 5:17

teacher of Israel and do not understand these things?"[31]

Likewise, Jesus astonished the congregation at His own synagogue in Nazareth by reading the appointed text for that Shabbat,

> The Spirit of the Lord is upon Me, because He anointed Me to preach the gospel [good news] to the poor. He has sent Me to proclaim release to the captives, and recovery of sight to the blind, to set free those who are oppressed, to proclaim the favorable year of the Lord.[32]

Astonishingly, He concluded by saying, "Today this Scripture has been fulfilled in your hearing."[33]   With this, He proclaimed the very inauguration and authorization of His messianic call!

Consider, if you will, that if it is true, as He Himself consistently affirmed, that He was "sent of the Father," what must the consequence of His rejection be to a people who *persist* in rejecting Him, as those to whom He was especially sent?   What a slight to the Father whose voice, according to the record, came from heaven over the transfigured Messiah, "This is My beloved Son…listen to Him!"[34]   For what reason do we disclaim this account? Can this be a fulfillment of the inspired warning foretold us by Moses?

> The Lord your God will raise up for you a prophet like me from among you, from your countrymen, you shall listen to him…and I will put My words in his mouth, and he shall speak to them all that I command him.   It shall come about that whoever will not listen to My words

---

[31] John 3:5-6,10
[32] Luke 4:18-19 (quoting from Isaiah 61:1)
[33] Ibid., v. 21
[34] Matthew 17:5b

which he shall speak in My name, I Myself will
require it of him[35]

What blessed provision have we also spurned *in
persisting in that same refusal* to consider Him who said, "I
came that they may have life, and have it abundantly."[36]

What true *Pesach* (Passover) can we have if He is, as
John the Baptist proclaimed Him to be, "Behold, the Lamb
of God who takes away the sin of the world!"[37] Could John
have been considering that: "…the life of the flesh is in the
blood, and I have given it to you on the altar to make
atonement for your souls; for it is the blood by reason of
the life that makes atonement"[38]? If there is no blood shed
to atone for our sins, what valid Yom Kippur, required by
the Law, remains to us after the destruction of the Temple,
priesthood, and sacrifices?

This being so, can rabbinically determined
"mitzvot"—fasting, and a day's Yom Kippur synagogue
attendance—be an acceptable substitute in the sight of
God? Or are these mere expediencies, conceived by well-
meaning men, upon the destruction of the Temple in 70
AD, which seemed to offer coherence and continuation for
a now dispersed nation? In this, they also avoided the only
other option, already chosen by tens of thousands of Jews,
who understood the sacrificial death of Yeshua Ha
Mashiach (Jesus the Christ) as God's once-and-for-all Yom
Kippur. These same alternatives confront us today!

---

[35] Deuteronomy 18:15, 18b-19
[36] John 10:10b
[37] John 1:29b
[38] Leviticus 17:11

The Consequences of Rejecting God

Jesus grieved, both as Messiah and Prophet, foreseeing the consequences that would befall us in our rejection of Him. He foresaw, not only the destruction of the Temple and the dispersal of the nation, but also the tragic events that would pursue us into the Diaspora.

> "And when He [Jesus] approached Jerusalem, He saw the city and wept over it, saying, "If you had known in this day, even you, the things which make for peace! But now they have been hidden from your eyes…and they will not leave in you one stone upon another, because you did not recognize the time of your visitation."[39]

Either the crucified Messiah was the once-and-for-all Atonement to which the biblical sacrifices had pointed, and for which purpose He said He had come, or the Jewish nation is left with the cruel dilemma of the Mosaic requirement rendered inoperable by the destruction of the Temple and the dispersal of the priesthood. This continues as an unresolved issue to this day.

Surely, then, the Jesus who warned of our being liable for every idle word we speak would not lightly exclaim, "…for unless you believe that I am He, you will die in your sins [i.e., without necessary atonement].[40]

Foreseeing the unspeakable anguish of such loss, as well as the prospect of terror of an endless torment, the divinely instructed apostle Paul proclaims, "For the wages of sin is death [eternal and irremediable separation from God], but the free gift of God is eternal life in Christ Jesus our Lord.[41]

---

[39] Luke 19: 41-42,44b
[40] John 8:24b
[41] Romans 6:23

Why, dear reader, if you have patiently borne with us thus far, should you *not* consider these things? What perceivable error do you find to justify rejecting them? However relativistic one's mindset, can God in His divine prerogative not insist upon a *scandal of particularity* centering in this One? What if that same One specifically fulfills the over 300 prophecies that speak of His birth, its time and location,[42] and His suffering, rejection, death and resurrection,[43] as well as His yet future and imminent return when, "...they will look on Me whom they have pierced"[44]? And learn that "the wounds between Your hands" were "those with which I was wounded in the house of My friends"[45]?

The New Testament confirms these prophetic themes when it declares, "...these [things] have been written so that you may believe that Jesus is the Christ, the Son of God; *and that believing* you may have life in His name.[46]

Yes, we know that Judaism does not believe that God has a Son.[47] But with all due respect, may we ask, what is this *Judaism?* Is it some sacrosanct entity *greater* than God, or rather, a compendium of rabbinical opinion framed

---

[42] Micah 5:2

[43] Isaiah 53

[44] Zechariah 12:10b

[45]Zechariah 13:6b (According to a literal rendering of the Masoretic text)

[46] John: 20:31. Emphasis mine

[47] This, in spite of the testimony of Psalm 2:7, "I will surely tell of the decree of the LORD: He said to Me, 'You are My Son, today I have begotten You.' "

Psalm 2:12, "Do homage to the Son, that He not become angry, and you perish in the way, for His wrath may soon be kindled. How blessed are all who take refuge in Him!" and Proverbs 30:4, "Who has ascended into heaven and descended? Who has gathered the wind in His fists? Who has wrapped the waters in His garment? Who has established all the ends of the earth? What is His name or His son's name? Surely you know!"

for over two thousand years in conscious opposition to, and repudiation of, the messianic claims of Jesus?[48] Let us be sure we do not invoke the Judaism of man to sidestep our obligation as *menschen* (responsible individuals) to consider issues of truth for which we are eternally liable.

Are we so persuaded that our traditional concept of God apprehends the full richness of biblical monotheism? What of a possible composite tri-unity, whose definition by men must always be less than its ineffable glory? Might God not be One [*Echad*], even as we are, made in His image—body, soul and spirit—and yet be One?

Many of us who are formed in the Jewish tradition will have to consider the words of Him who was also the Author of the renowned Sermon on the Mount: "He who has seen Me has seen the Father."[49] He spoke repeatedly of having come from the Father, and that "He would depart out of this world to the Father...that He had come forth from God and was going back to God."[50] Ought this not to give one, as it has us, sufficient reason to re-examine one's conception of God?

---

[48] We are aware of, and deplore, the painful and forced confrontations to which our people have been subjected under "Christendom." We appreciate the rabbinical defense of Judaism against the encroachment of what was rightly understood then as an apparent pagan idolatry. God forbid that this book be thus misconstrued as being in keeping with that ungodly coercion. Nevertheless, "God would have all men to be converted," that is, to voluntarily and totally turn to Himself in spirit and in truth. Our effort here is to challenge and stir the reader to that consideration.

[49] John 14:9b

[50] John 13:1b, 3f

The Consequences of Believing God

Without question, if these things are true, it will turn one's world upside down. All our trusted categories will necessarily be challenged. Except we be willing to bear *that* consequence, how shall our allegiance be ultimately tested in the foremost commandment to "love the Lord, our God, with all our heart, soul, mind and strength"?

Will you yourself not ask the God of Abraham, Isaac and Jacob about the crucial claims Jesus made for Himself? Will you not choose to rise above that instinctive, historically-conditioned enmity to His name? Scripture soberly informs us, "There is no other name under heaven that has been given among men by which we must be saved."[51] Will you not trust and test the Word of God by *acting* upon it?

> For the Scripture says, "Whoever believes in Him will not be disappointed. For there is no distinction between Jew and Greek [Gentile]; for the same Lord is Lord of all, abounding in riches for all who call on Him.[52]

Even the famous "doubting" Thomas said, "Unless I see in His hands the imprint of the nails, and put my finger into the place of the nails, and put my hand into His side, I will not believe."[53] But upon seeing the resurrected Christ, he let out the astonished gasp, "My Lord and my God!"[54] Jesus, forsaking a once-and-for-all opportunity to squelch a preposterous and blasphemous exaggeration, acknowledged it as being perfectly appropriate to Himself, adding, "Blessed are they who did not see, and yet believed."[55]

---

[51] Acts 4:12b
[52] Romans 10:11-12
[53] John 20:25b
[54] Ibid v. 28b
[55] Ibid., v. 29b

Is it not significant and revealing that the best of Roman Law, coupled with the best of Jewish piety, put to a cruel death the long-awaited Object of our faith? With our scant and pitiful consciousness of sin—what need for atonement then?—we ought to ponder that God, knowing how sin disguises itself, became Himself our victim, in order to reveal, as nothing else could, the inexorable truth of *our* condition!   Tragically, not only were we too blind to recognize Him, but as a nation were sufficiently offended and threatened by Him, making His removal by death a *necessity*! As the Scripture says, "…like one from whom men hide their face He was despised, and we did not esteem Him."[56]

What person or nation can be absolved from such sin as this? If this be so, what passage of time can in any way mitigate our personal and corporate guilt? Our defiant declaration, "His [Jesus'] blood shall be on us and on our children,"[57] has haunted us throughout our history more than we can know.

If He be the Son of God, "very God and very Man," as ancient creeds declare, we have committed an appalling sin. Not the sin of a failed moment's error, mind you, but rather the summation of all sin, chronic and ages old, and repeated again in a Judaism that, to this day, *prefers* the rulings of a rabbinical "elite," and of "ideas comfortably usable in modernity." Against this, ironically, stands the timeless *Shema* of Deuteronomy 6:4-6 that either defrocks Jesus as ultimate blasphemer, or shows Him to be the very One for whom, in the wisdom of God, the ancient creed was given! As our painful history testifies only too well, "Be sure your sin will find you out."[58]

Have we been the "Cain" to this "Abel"—moved to murderous envy of a "Son" of the Father more virtuous

---

[56] Isaiah 53:3b
[57] Matthew 27:25
[58] Numbers 32:23

than we, whose greater and altogether righteous sacrifice, accepted by the Father, leaves our own sacrifice unaccepted and *unacceptable*?[59]   Ours, the inept product of our own sweat and industry; His, the ultimate, acceptable blood-sacrifice, satisfying the Holiness of God, which cannot be placated by *anything* mankind can humanly or religiously provide!

Have we, like Cain, become fugitives and vagabonds in the earth, hidden from the face of God, *marked,* but all too often *not* spared?   The comparison is altogether too close to be comfortable!   Ought we not be stricken with sorrow, seeing our likeness to that first murderer?   May we not bear, ever so remotely, any resemblance to Cain's penalty!   Better yet, "Whoever calls on the name of the LORD will be delivered [saved]."[60]

> But what does it say? "The word is near you, in your mouth and in your heart"—that is, the word of faith which we are preaching, that if you confess with your mouth Jesus as Lord, and believe in your heart that God raised Him from the dead, you will be saved.[61]

Thus, the Apostle Paul, Hebrew of the Hebrews, did not forsake his Jewishness.   Nor do we, in proclaiming the good news of our Messiah, "...for it is the *power of God* for salvation to everyone who believes; *to the Jew first* and also to the Greek."[62]

---

[59] See the account in Genesis 4.

[60] Joel 2:32a

[61] Romans 10:8-10

[62] Romans 1:16b. Emphases mine

A Final Prophetic Consideration

Some may ask, why must there be a soon-coming "time of Jacob's trouble," as prophesied by Jeremiah[63]—a global anti-Semitism threatening to exceed even that of the Nazi Holocaust? Because, truth to tell, are we not still Jacob—meaning "schemer"—and not yet Israel—meaning "prince with God"? Is there not a Man waiting for us, with whom we must ourselves wrestle till *daybreak*—in a *night* that must come, and hastens even now? Are we not barred from full possession again of the Land of our fathers by the inveterate "Esau," who would again have our life? Is there not a final drama of reconciliation with a vengeful brother, which we must play out first by confronting God in a Man?

But, like our father Jacob, whose heel-grasping nature we yet painfully retain, for all our success in the Diaspora, our "pillowed head" is once again upon a stone! And yet, God is in *that* place, however "dreadful" it be, and though we know it not, it is the gate to heaven! Pour oil upon that stone though you will, and promise the Jacob's tenth though you will, it is but a token of the total consecration that alone makes of a Jacob an *Israel*. Is it not for *this* that God waits?

He waits at that threshold of blessedness as the Man we have too long avoided. But there is no entry into that blessedness till we shall say like Jacob, "I will not let *You* go unless *You* bless me."[64] It is this stubborn specificity of God, coming in the form of His own choosing, with which we must grapple! Only the recognition of the face of God in *that* scandalous Man can break our inveterate, self-determining, and self-affirming Jacob-pride. Jesus alone, face-to-face, turns us into the Israel of God!

---

[63] See chapter 30:7
[64] Genesis 32:26. Emphases mine

So "send over all" that we have, divide our substance into two bands, devise every Jacob scheme that we will; it will not save us from the outraged brother who brings his "four hundred with him"!   That Man, whom we have struggled so long to avoid—only *His* touch at the hip socket of our Jacob self-sufficiency and confidence can "cripple" us and make us, for the first time, a worshipping, lame supplicant at His Altar—the altar of El-Elohe-Israel!

Out of "a broken and contrite heart," which He will not despise, issues the authentic, self-surrendering worship that transfigures Jacob the usurper into a servant-son—now rightly named *Israel*.[65]   Reconciled to God, as a son to his father, we will, with Him, overcome every enmity, however ancient and bitter.

All of our Jacob-striving propensity to obtain by our wit and cunning is, ironically, what God all along intended as our inheritance—had we but known Him as we ought, and received it in all humility at His hand! Break, break, O sons of Jacob. The Father of our fathers, the Ancient of Days, the Lord of Glory, and the Savior of Israel, awaits our worship. And till that worship come, what possession of our inheritance, what priestly service to "bless all the families of the earth"—especially of the kin of Esau and Ishmael—can there be?[66]   Our neighbor, with whom we have striven, needs now to be blessed by an Israel that indeed is Israel, and who has at last acknowledged: "Blessed is the one who comes in the name of the Lord."[67]

That blessedness is worth our every present travail. Do we recognize the press of God in the anti-Semitism raised once again to haunt us? Our false, secular and non-biblical hopes have not, and cannot, save us. The sins of our fathers, being also our own, pursue us in every generation, awaiting their acknowledgment and repentant

---

[65] See Psalms 51:17
[66] See Genesis 12:3
[67] Psalms 118:26a

forsaking.[68]   Our sins have required Him to turn His face from us for the "moment" but with abundant mercy will He receive and restore us and make us His own—to the everlasting praise of His glory.

A Prayer:

Lord, grant mercy to me, the reader in this once-and-for-all moment. You know well how every power in the world has conspired to shut you out of my consideration. Grant me, in this moment, a release from all that has barred me, as a Jew, from calling upon your Name. Give me some measure of the same humility that You Yourself bore nakedly in that public shame on the cross. Thank you for making this crisis of decision possible for me. In Jesus' holy, and till now, untried name, I ask. Save me! Amen.

---

[68] See Leviticus 26:39-42

OTHER BOOKS by Art Katz

REALITY: THE HOPE OF GLORY
with Phil Chomak

The four messages in this book address the Spirit-led life of men who were committed to the vision of Christ being seen in the glory of His people. It is therefore a bold challenge to every lesser version of Christian life, and a powerful inspiration to those who will not settle for less than the true meaning of life as a disciple of Christ. Paperback, 156 pages.

THE SPIRIT OF TRUTH
with Paul Volk

Into this age of religious pretension, exaggeration and deception, Art brings a deep, incisive probing into the nature of truth. This book calls the church back to its essential identity as the "ground and pillar of truth," without which, all its activity is a sham. Every lover and guardian of truth will find this an insightful and demanding book. Paperback, 101 pages.

THE HOLOCAUST: WHERE WAS GOD? – *An inquiry into the biblical roots of tragedy.*

In a daring hypothesis, the author turns to the ancient Hebrew scriptures as the key of interpretation to one of the most catastrophic events of modern times—the Jewish Holocaust of World War II. Challenging both the agnostic secularist as well as the religiously-minded, Art compels a searching re-appraisal of one's deepest convictions. In this examination of that ultimate tragedy, the issue of God as God is brought courageously to the forefront of our modern consideration as few books have attempted to do. Paperback, 91 pages.

APOSTOLIC FOUNDATIONS

In his penetrating manner, Art captures the flavor and essential meaning of the church's holy foundation—Christ Jesus Himself being the Cornerstone. Art points out that a church with apostolic foundations is a body of people whose central impulse is a radical and total jealousy for the glory of God. It was so at the church's inception, and needs to be so at its conclusion. Paperback, 272 pages.

BEN ISRAEL – ODYSSEY OF A MODERN JEW

Written as a literal journal, Art recounts his experience as an atheist and former Marxist being apprehended by a God whom he was not seeking. Taking a leave of absence from the teaching profession, his search for the ultimate meaning of life ended significantly and symbolically in Jerusalem. The message of this book has been powerfully used to bring other of Art's Jewish kinsmen to the faith of their fathers. Paperback, 149 pages.

THE TEMPTATIONS OF CHRIST – A CALL TO SONSHIP AND MATURITY

The scriptures indicate that Jesus was led into the wilderness in the *fullness* of the Spirit, but came out of that testing place in the *power* of the Spirit. The author examines the necessary progression in our Christian life without which we will never be able to open the "synagogue scrolls" of our localities and speak with the grace and power that alone gives testimony to the resurrection of the Lord Jesus. Paperback, 56 pages.